FLOWERS OF TIME

Flowers of Time

ON POSTAPOCALYPTIC FICTION

MARK PAYNE

PRINCETON UNIVERSITY PRESS
PRINCETON & OXFORD

Copyright © 2020 by Princeton University Press

Requests for permission to reproduce material from this work should be sent to permissions@press.princeton.edu

Published by Princeton University Press
41 William Street, Princeton, New Jersey 08540
6 Oxford Street, Woodstock, Oxfordshire OX20 1TR

press.princeton.edu

All Rights Reserved

Library of Congress Cataloging-in-Publication Data
Names: Payne, Mark, 1967– author.
Title: Flowers of time : on post-apocalyptic fiction / Mark Payne.
Description: Princeton : Princeton University Press, [2020] | Includes index.
Identifiers: LCCN 2020002321 (print) | LCCN 2020002322 (ebook) | ISBN 9780691205427 (hardback ; acid-free paper) | ISBN 9780691205946 (paperback ; acid-free paper) | ISBN 9780691206400 (ebook)
Subjects: LCSH: Apocalypse in literature. | Apocalyptic fiction—History and criticism. | End of the world in literature. | Dystopias—History.
Classification: LCC PN56.A69 P39 2020 (print) | LCC PN56.A69 (ebook) | DDC 809.3/9372—dc23
LC record available at https://lccn.loc.gov/2020002321
LC ebook record available at https://lccn.loc.gov/2020002322

British Library Cataloging-in-Publication Data is available

Editorial: Anne Savarese and Jenny Tan
Production Editorial: Ellen Foos
Jacket/Cover Design: Layla Mac Rory
Production: Brigid Ackerman
Publicity: Alyssa Sanford and Amy Stewart
Copyeditor: Daniel Simon

Jacket art: Jim Denomie, *Spiritual Landscape,* 2017. Courtesy of the artist and Bockley Gallery

This book has been composed in Arno

Printed on acid-free paper. ∞

Printed in the United States of America

10 9 8 7 6 5 4 3 2 1

"The very flower of Time, which never bloomed before, and never by any possibility can bloom again."

—NATHANIEL HAWTHORNE, *ENGLISH NOTEBOOKS*, JULY 26TH [1857], SUNDAY, OLD TRAFFORD

CONTENTS

Acknowledgments ix

Introduction: Postapocalyptic Pastoral   1

1   The Apocalyptic Cosmos   37

2   The Persistence of Memory   64

3   Survivalist Anthropology   128

Conclusion: Landscape with Figures   163

Works Cited   173

Index   181

ACKNOWLEDGMENTS

I AM GRATEFUL to many friends for their intellectual companionship while working on this book. At the University of Chicago, Deme Kasimis of the Department of Political Science offered invaluable recommendations on Rousseau and marronage. Cody Jones of the Department of Comparative Literature was an ever-present interlocutor on theory, fiction, and everything in between. I am also grateful to Andrei Pop of the Committee on Social Thought for sharing with me his boundless knowledge of the wide world of speculative fiction.

Conversations on Native American history with Jonathan Lear, and with Scott and Urban Bear Don't Walk, continue to resonate in this book. Urban has now passed on, but I will always be grateful to him for sharing his thoughts with me on the walks, drives, and hospital visits we took when I was visiting Crow country.

Sam Cooper of Bard High School in Queens helped me see connections between classical literature and modern speculative fiction that I would not have seen without him, and I learned a lot from his own work in these areas. Brooke Holmes of Princeton University encouraged me to think harder about what I was doing, as she always does. In England, Tom Phillips of the University of Manchester, David Fearn and Victoria Rimell of the University of Warwick, and Miriam Leonard of University College London lent receptive ears to the lines of kinship I was trying to establish.

Audiences at UCLA, Florida State University, the University of Manchester, the Boghossian Foundation, Johns Hopkins

University, and the Franke Institute for the Humanities at the University of Chicago helped me move forward with their lively discussions of papers I presented at various stages of this project.

This book was conceived, and a first draft written, during a yearlong leave from the Division of Humanities at the University of Chicago. I am thankful to Deans Martha Roth and Anne Robertson for the support that made it possible.

Many thanks too to Anne Savarese at Princeton University Press for taking the manuscript on and for recruiting the two excellent readers whose insights and suggestions made it a much better book than it would otherwise have been.

An earlier version of part of chapter 1 was published as "Postapocalyptic Humanism in Hesiod, Mary Shelley, and Olaf Stapledon" in *Classical Receptions* 12, no. 1 (2020): 91–108. My thanks to the editors and readers of the journal for their enthusiasm.

Last but very much not least, thanks to my wife and children for putting up with some difficult times during my work on this project. One of the claims I make in the book is that postapocalyptic fiction is a cheerful genre, but I don't know that any of you would have guessed that while I was working on it. Thanks to Laura, Carolyn, and Alice for all your love and support.

FLOWERS OF TIME

INTRODUCTION

Postapocalyptic Pastoral

THE APOCALYPSE is everywhere right now. In beach reads and blue chip fiction; in comic books and young adult novels; in streaming TV shows, major motion pictures, and ironic art-house cinema. Wherever you look, small groups of beleaguered survivors are banding together to outsmart zombies or crazed survivalists, and generally doing their best to get by on a planet ravaged by pollution, consumerism, and reckless resource extraction.

Critics have begun to roll their eyes in the face of this abundance. In "What's the matter with dystopia?" Ursula Heise echoes biologist Peter Kareiva in questioning the value of the current outpouring of apocalyptic imaginings. What does such "apocaholism" accomplish, other than encouraging us to turn our backs on the difficult work of fighting global inequity and ecological destruction, so that we can fantasize instead about the "hipster DIY and maker culture" that might come after the end of days?[1]

For all its present ubiquity, apocalyptic fiction is an ancient form of the human imagination. It includes the biblical story of Noah, *The Epic of Gilgamesh*, and the *Works and Days* of the ancient Greek poet Hesiod as well as a vast array of modern examples. A basic distinction can be made in this archive between apocalyptic fictions, which focus on the end of days itself, and postapocalyptic fictions, which imagine the life that human beings

---

1. Heise (2015).

might lead after the apocalyptic event has passed. In this book, I focus on the latter: large-scale works of literary fiction that stage how new forms of life emerge from catastrophe, how survivors adapt to the altered conditions of existence, and the various ways in which the past asserts its claims on them—both the immediate past of the world that is lost as well as the deep past of prehistory and the anthropological imagination that returns with this loss.

Postapocalyptic fiction is political theory in fictional form. Instead of producing arguments in favor of a particular form of life, it shows what it would be like to live that life. This is its mode of persuasion. Modern postapocalyptic fiction begins with Mary Shelley's *The Last Man* (1826), which stages the return of small-scale agrarianism in the aftermath of catastrophe, but this aspect of postapocalyptic fiction is not local to modernity. Shelley presents the agricultural survivalism of the ancient Greek poet Hesiod (eighth century BCE) as the model for the postapocalyptic social thought of her novel, and for ancient philosophers, Hesiod's poetry was a regular starting point for thinking about the foundations of social order and cohesion.

Hesiod was the first Greek thinker to offer a decisive, first-person articulation of the ideas of justice, obligation, and human relationality that went by the name of *dike* (δίκη). And while the mainstream of Greek political thought centered on the polis as the form of life in which these aspirations could best be realized, an alternative tradition looked to poetry for its vision of the superiority of nonpolis life. In Hesiod's account of the Golden Age, an earlier version of humankind once inhabited the earth on better terms than human beings do now. These humans were destroyed by the gods, but their existence was real, and poetry recalls it and appeals to it, as the hope for a form of life to come.

By looking at the ways in which modern postapocalyptic fiction reframes and restages its ancient claims to attention, we can better understand its current popularity. Postapocalyptic fiction imagines forms of human freedom, sociality, and capability outside the discourse of normative theory. It populates the gaps where political imagination is lacking and shows us forms of life that are materially and culturally impoverished in comparison to what came before the apocalyptic event, but more deeply satisfying as a result. Once the immediate consequences of the apocalyptic event have been lived through, forms of life emerge that afford the protagonists a more varied use of their own capabilities than was possible for them before.

Postapocalyptic fiction is by definition catastrophic. The forms of life it imagines can only emerge from disaster on a global scale. They are not, and cannot be, the outcome of a deliberate crafting of social realities that has their installation in view. They can only emerge from a lack of political deliberation, out of the need-based sociality that characterizes human association in the aftermath of a catastrophic event that human beings did not intend. The apocalyptic event affords human beings a way of beginning over that circumvents their own best intentions for themselves with regard to their form of life.

It is a fundamental premise of postapocalyptic fiction that human beings cannot grasp what is best for themselves through rational deliberation within the social circumstances that prevail at the time of the apocalyptic event. Their minds are deformed by their form of life, which must therefore be reset by a power external to themselves. The apocalyptic event rescales human aspirations for a better life from illusory macrosocial goals to the level of individual capabilities grounded in the human body. Once the survivors discover what they are capable of, they understand that any future form of social life must afford human beings the use of this expanded set of capabilities if it is to retain its appeal. This is a lesson that could not have been learned in the more complex forms of social organization that preceded the apocalyptic event because it cannot be learned in any other way than through experience.

Robinson Crusoe has been a persistent model for postapocalyptic fiction in this regard. Virginia Woolf puts her finger on the relationship between unforeseen occupations, unsuspected capabilities, and the emergence of new forms of mental life in Defoe's novel: "To dig, to bake, to plant, to build—how serious these simple occupations are; hatchets, scissors, logs, axes—how beautiful these simple objects become."[2] As Crusoe focuses on the work of survival, his new occupations reward him with new forms of mental life that he could not have experienced or anticipated in society. Ordinary objects reveal a hidden beauty. The world around him is newly absorbing, profoundly worthy of attention, because his activities disclose it to him in new and unsuspected ways. These are not forms of mentation he could have created for himself in his old life. He had to be forcibly expelled from that life for them to come into being. Previously, he had plans, goals, ambitions, dreams. His life was an attempt to catch up with an image of himself he projected into the future, an anticipation of the person he would become once he had broken with his father, traveled the world, and made his fortune. Now he is all together again in the place where he is.

In *Capital*, Karl Marx derides *Robinson Crusoe* as an inane fantasy beloved of British political economists. Crusoe fails to understand that the new forms of mental life that come to him from his new occupations are merely the return to himself of forms of mentation that are variously distributed among the productive members of his own society, which is founded upon division of labor. Because Crusoe fails to grasp the relationship between the division of labor and the distribution of distinctive forms of mentation, Marx dismisses his mental life as a symptom of alienation that is in no way remediated by his time on the island.[3]

The philosophic hero of Marx's analysis is Aristotle, "the great investigator who was the first to analyse the value-form, like so many other forms of thought, society, and nature."[4] More explicitly still in the *Grundrisse*, Marx's dismissal of the Robinsonade is

2. Woolf (1932) 57.
3. Marx (1990) 169–70.
4. Marx (1990) 151.

formulated as Aristotelian fundamentalism about the impossibility of being human outside the polis: "The human being is in the most literal sense of the word a ζῷον πολιτικόν, not merely a gregarious animal, but an animal which can individuate itself only in the midst of society." As we shall see, Aristotle's position on these questions was not the orthodoxy Marx takes it to be in classical antiquity. In *The Life of Greece*, Aristotle's own student Dicaearchus rejected the political ontology of the *Politics* that Marx invokes here, calling instead for a return to the poets for a true disclosure of the relationship between occupation and mentation in life outside and prior to the polis.

Marx cannot see beyond Aristotle's political ontology, and, like Aristotle, he does not think the life of premodern people is worthy of serious consideration. He mocks Rousseau, Smith, and Ricardo for seeking the origin of social cohesion in "the isolated hunter and fisherman" who chooses to integrate himself into a larger social group, and in *The German Ideology*, he refers to the "sheep-like or tribal consciousness" that precedes political life as such.[5] He never considers that group cohesion in societies that precede agricultural dependence is grounded in a potential for individual self-sufficiency which allows being together to be a choice, not an obligation, for its members. This is not to misunderstand the social contract as a historical event in the lives of such peoples, but to grasp how social belonging actually works in their societies, and why.

In chapter 3, I consider the staging of postreservation life in the novels of D'Arcy McNickle and James Welch, where the elimination of a social bond grounded in each individual's capacity for survival constitutes a primary obstacle for younger indigenous people in adapting to new forms of social life. Subsistence activities are not simply the alternation of pastimes that Marx imagines in *The German Ideology*, in his Marie Antoinette–like vision of a world in which one will "hunt in the morning, fish in the

5. Marx (1993) 83–84; Marx (1998) 50.

afternoon, rear cattle in the evening, criticise after dinner, just as I have in mind, without ever becoming hunter, fisherman, shepherd or critic."[6] The premodern capabilities to which postapocalyptic fiction looks mean actually being able to do things for yourself, without having to rely on others to do them for you. In the case of hunting and fishing, this includes, minimally, knowing what kinds of animals to kill at any given time, how to skin and clean them properly, how to distribute the meat and hides, and how to dispose of the waste.[7] Without this knowledge, "hunting" is just target practice with animals.

In navigating between Woolf and Marx, we should bear in mind that *Robinson Crusoe* is already an ancient story type when Defoe makes use of it. In Sophocles' *Philoctetes*, the Greek soldier who gives the play its name is marooned by his comrades on the island of Lemnos where he must survive for himself using a bow entrusted to him by Heracles. The story is set at the time of the Trojan War, and Sophocles imagines the island as devoid of human beings, which it never was in the historical period. *Philoctetes* is an ancient speculative fiction that imagines how it might be possible for the life of a single human being to encompass successive eras of human life. The years that Philoctetes spends on the island afford him new ways of relating to the nonhuman species that are his companions, and he hails them in song as the play comes to an end and he returns to the civilization of the polis.[8]

---

6. Marx (1998) 53.

7. Cf. Le Guin (2019) 493: Postapocalyptic hunting looks like indigenous hunting because that's what hunting is. Or as she observes in her essay "A Non-Euclidean View of California as a Cold Place to Be," Le Guin (2019) 715: "The world where robots do the work while the human beings sit back and play . . . were always satirical works."

8. Stabler (2013) 38 notes "the address to the earth" as the ground of commonality in Hazlitt's view of Philoctetes as the precursor to Crusoe: in this, "the most beautiful of all the Greek tragedies," Hazlitt observes, "the very beatings of his heart become audible in the eternal silence that surrounds him." As I argue in chapter 2, the return to subsistence that Philoctetes and Crusoe experience brings with it a reawakening

For all its associations with the economic theory of early capitalism, the Robinsonade predates *Robinson Crusoe* by millennia,[9] and its first clear example in Greek literature is already an exploration of the relationship between occupation and mentation under altered conditions of survival. The appeal of the Robinsonade, including *Robinson Crusoe* itself, unfolds in the gap between what the protagonists themselves make of their situation and what we can imagine making of it for ourselves—or what we can imagine it making of us. Protagonists and reader are alike on trial, and if one or another of them fails the test, this does not invalidate the diagnostic value of the procedure.

The *Oxford English Dictionary* defines mentation as "mental activity, esp. seen as a physiological process." It is this tight but elusive, quasimedical connection between the life of the body and the life of the mind to which I adhere in this book. Mentation thematizes the relationship between the two without taking a position on which aspects of mental life are actually or properly conscious, and which unconscious. According to *Mosby's Medical Dictionary*, mentation is "any mental activity, including conscious and unconscious processes."[10] It recognizes that the balance between the two is fluid and that physical activities which are not themselves mental in the first instance affect this balance. It also thereby implies that the origin of particular forms of mentation may be impossible for its human subjects to discern or to deliberately produce for themselves.

Ursula Le Guin's *Always Coming Home* offers an excellent example of what I mean here by mentation. Stone Telling, a member of the Kesh, one of the novel's postapocalyptic Californian

---

of what Rousseau calls "the sentiment of existence." See Rousseau (1979) 89; Rousseau (1997) 161.

9. As I discuss in my conclusion, Csicsery-Ronay (2003) 232 recognizes the transhistorical components of the story type in his naming of its primary "diegetic agents."

10. Mosby (2013) 1122.

peoples, describes the relationship between occupation and mentation in their daily lives:

> Nothing we do is better than the work of handmind. When mind uses itself without the hands it runs the circle and may go too fast; even speech using the voice only may go too fast. The hand that shapes the mind into clay or written word slows thought to the gait of things and lets it be subject to accident and time. Purity is on the edge of evil, they say.[11]

Stone Telling describes an activity that, even with the initial stumbling block "handmind," we instinctively label "craft." However, her final sentence pushes this hasty self-recognition away from us. Handmind belongs to another form of life, with other origins than our own, and we have to feel our way into it gradually, comparing the relationships between occupation and mentation that it stages with those that we know from our own world.

In *The Discourse on Inequality*, Rousseau argued that the indigenous inhabitant of the New World carried "all of himself along with him," whereas the aspiration of the modern European was to outsource the occupations of natural life to others, and invest himself in ambitions for the future.[12] Rousseau repurposes a version of wisdom that Cicero attributes to the Greek sage Bias of Priene: "Everything that is mine I take along with me."[13] But whereas for the Stoics the possession of inalienable virtue is the ground of contentment, for Rousseau it is retaining the use of capabilities that are all too easily alienated and forgotten. As he documents at length in his accompanying notes, the inhabitants of the New World have bodily capabilities that modern Europeans can scarcely account for or acknowledge as common human powers.

It is the experience of putting themselves together again as subjects of natural life that gives the protagonists of postapocalyptic

---

11. Le Guin (2019) 210.
12. Rousseau (1997) 135.
13. Cicero, *Paradoxes of the Stoics*, 1.8: *Omnia mea mecum porto*.

fiction their confidence that they know what they are doing when they enter into new forms of social life. We see how new practices of daily life produce new kinds of mentation for them. Beauty, seriousness, and commitment emerge from engagement with the things of the world, rather than by separating oneself from them in deliberate acts of contemplation. Interiority and exteriority are not set against each other but grow together in new forms of relatedness. Understanding what has been restored to them through their occupations, postapocalyptic survivors are circumspect about social obligations that would require them to surrender what they have recovered.

In its disclosure of what becomes available to human beings in the work of living on, postapocalyptic fiction points back to organic meanings of *apokalypsis* that are obscured in the word's uptake by eschatological Christianity. As well as the deliberate removal of a veil, the Greek word names the unfolding of a flower from its protective sheath, as what had been hidden from view emerges into sight through a nonvolitional process. Postapocalyptic fiction runs these two senses of apocalypse together. On one hand, the apocalyptic event is what comes to human beings from the outside, projecting them outside their accustomed forms of life in ways they could not have anticipated. On the other, it allows capabilities that were occluded in their previous form of life to emerge naturally into the light of day. Like plants that can only reseed themselves in the aftermath of fire, postapocalyptic fiction imagines an ecology of human survival in which the best possibilities of humankind can only make their appearance again after large-scale events of destruction. As Nathaniel Hawthorne intuited in his visit to the Manchester Arts Exhibition, to see a relic of antiquity uprooted from its native ground is to see it as "the very flower of Time, which never bloomed before, and never by any possibility can bloom again"—unless by some chance the conditions of its original efflorescence are restored.

Shelley's *The Last Man* (1826) details the survival efforts of a dwindling group of human beings who live on in the aftermath of a plague that eventually reduces the global population to zero. Shelley scales up the fundamental relationship between occupation and mentation that is staged so vividly in *Robinson Crusoe* from the level of the individual to the level of the group. Rather than one man alone experiencing the new forms of mental life that emerge from the activities of survival, Shelley stages the thinking of a community as it emerges together into these new forms of mentation.

In the aftermath of the global pandemic in Shelley's novel, there is a return of the thought world of Greco-Roman antiquity. The survivors do not choose this form of mentation for themselves; it comes about automatically as a condition of their reversion to local forms of agricultural production. As hierarchical, large-scale civilization disappears and is replaced by basic agrarianism in which everyone participates equally, Greek mythology reasserts itself as the natural expression of their new form of life. If we are tempted to discount the revelations of *Robinson Crusoe* as due at least in part to the trauma of isolation, Shelley's survivors are a group that lives and works together. Plurality functions as a kind of fictional control on the novel's experiment with the emergence of new forms of mental life. If Shelley's survivors are deluded or traumatized, they are at least experiencing a collective hallucination rather than the miseries of involuntary solitude.

The Last Man is closely concerned with forms of inhabitation in local settings, and it assiduously documents the correlation between survival facts and survivor mentality. The inspiration that Shelley found for her project in the Greek poet Hesiod is recorded in the novel in the form of several long citations from his work (see chapter 1). Two poems by Hesiod of about one thousand lines each survive, along with fragments of a number of others. *Theogony* is about the gods—their origins, conflicts, and prerogatives. *Works and Days* is about human beings—what they do all day, and what they should be doing instead.

In keeping with its focus on the possibilities for human occupations, *Works and Days* also contains an account of how the present version of humankind is only the most recent in a series of human creations, and how these other versions of humankind lived in the past. According to Hesiod, the gods have destroyed and remade human beings several times. There were versions of humankind he calls gold, silver, and bronze. These were followed by the heroes and demigods of legend who immediately preceded our own iron humanity, the worst in every way of all the humankinds to have existed so far: less strong, less capable, and less just, to name only a few of its shortcomings in comparison with those who came before.

Human beings have always had to live with the enmity of the gods hanging over them. There was no consistent reason for the gods' previous annihilations of humankind, and human beings in the present are rightly understood as postapocalyptic survivors. And as the least pleasing outcome of all the divine interventions into the matter of human life, the destruction of the present iteration of humankind is likely to be imminent. The fate of humanity resembles the Noah story, but without righteousness necessarily being the deciding factor in whether or not the gods allow human beings to persist in their present version.

Hesiod recalls that previous generations of humankind inhabited the earth on better terms than we do. More capable in themselves and more favored by the gods, they lived more easily and more justly, doing less harm to one another and to other living beings than the generation of iron whose existence is defined by competition in the struggle to survive. What connects human beings in the present to these previous generations is the transmitted genealogical knowledge that things were once better than they are now. Hesiod posits a continuous underlying humanness in the experience of living with this knowledge, and the will to persist as human in spite of it. A human being is whoever has to learn how to live as best she can by pitting her knowledge of the lifeworld and her determination to survive against the human indifference or divine hostility that would cut her existence short.

Works and Days is the text of Hesiod with which Shelley is chiefly occupied as she crafts her own narrative of human beings' ultimately unsuccessful efforts at postapocalyptic survival in *The Last Man*. In chapter 1, "The Apocalyptic Cosmos," I examine how she refashions Hesiod's search for a continuous ground of humanness that persists through catastrophic transformations of the foundations of social life. Hesiod's Zeus periodically brings humankind to an end, and *Works and Days* consists not just of survival instructions but of ontological reflection on what it means for human beings to have to repeatedly rediscover themselves as such in the occupations of survival. Likewise, Shelley's Nature brings humanity to an end, and her survivors discover the possibility that their lives together could have been other than they were or thought they had to be. The forms of sociality under which they lived previously were not decisive expressions of their humanity, and the return to shared agricultural labor affords them a vision of the social, ecological, and divine relationships that might have been available to them instead. In the time that remains to them, they experience a more proximate relationship with the gods of Nature who afford them the means of survival.

Shelley's critics saw willful cruelty toward humankind in *The Last Man*, and her impersonal Nature is a difficult substitute for the divine hostility to human life that the Greeks called *phthonos* (φθόνος). *Phthonos* is ill-will or malice. It is often occasioned by the good fortune of others, but not always. The gods are also subject to *phthonos*, even toward human beings, whom they have no reason to envy. It is possible to experience animosity toward the wretched precisely because they are wretched, and the persistent, but variously motivated, hostility of Hesiod's gods toward the various iterations of humankind reflects the range of affective positions that lie behind this term as a purposive behavior.

Shelley brackets the question of motive in the destruction of humankind and makes herself a proxy of Nature in bringing the era of human occupation of the earth to an end. Her narrative anticipates future destruction at the hands of Nature, rather than recalling past enmity of the gods, and so raises troubling questions about the new forms of mentation her survivors discover in the aftermath of catastrophe. Is the return of the gods they experience a traumatic delusion, a collective equivalent of Crusoe's traumatized absorption in the work of survival? And if they are happy, does it really matter?

How human beings relate to cosmic forces that produce drastic transformations in their physical being and form of life is a fundamental preoccupation of the twentieth-century English writer of speculative fiction Olaf Stapledon. In his best-known novels, *Last and First Men* and *Star Maker*, Stapledon offers contrasting versions of the successive remaking of humankind as it unfolds against the massive timescales of cosmic duration. In *Last and First Men*, eighteen generations of humankind are surveyed from the present until their eventual destruction some two billion years in the future, with a view to what grounds the continuity of their species being. Here, Stapledon engages with postapocalyptic fiction's project of understanding what it is to be a human being through the relationship between occupation and mentation. Through all their various transformations, his generations of humankind are what they do. In *Star Maker*, he reframes this project as a journey toward the figure in whom these transformations originate. He resets the inquiry into humanness on a different basis, as the capacity of the human mind to grasp human transformation as adaptation to cosmic events that are rightly understood both as impersonal processes and as the willed activities of a personal being that human beings can encounter as such.

Hesiod, Mary Shelley, and Olaf Stapledon all subscribe to some version of an immediate relationship between occupation and mentation, and all three are also committed to a higher-level ontological formulation of humanness in response to it. Something lasting can be said about humanness by understanding how human beings come to recognize themselves through their occupations. In chapters 2 and 3, I consider how other authors of postapocalyptic fiction prioritize one or another of these commitments, asserting either the immediacy of the relationship between occupation and mentation without the need for higher-level ontological accounting, or imagining such accounting as itself a vital survival skill that must be ready to hand before the apocalyptic event, and continuously honed in the life that comes after it.

Chapter 2, "The Persistence of Memory," surveys the return of historical forms of life in postapocalyptic fiction after *The Last Man*. These include simple agrarianism and foraging, hunting and gathering, or some combination of the two, and they require human beings to make use of capabilities that were dormant or occluded in the civilization that disappeared with the apocalyptic event but which flourish in postapocalyptic life. As occupation determines mentation, the survivors fade back into the forms of life of the peoples who preceded them on their terrain, whether these are the neomedieval tribes of Richard Jefferies's *After London* (1885), the warring clans of Cicely Hamilton's *Theodore Savage* (1922), the Stone Age hunters of Leslie Mitchell's *Three Go Back* (1932) and *Gay Hunter* (1934), or the indigenous Americans of George Stewart's *Earth Abides* (1949) and Jean Hegland's *Into the Forest* (1996).

This is an apocalypse on trial. The reader gets to test out postapocalyptic life and see if she likes it. Sometimes this test has the form of an ordeal. Could she endure what it would take to get to a future in which the survivors are happier than she is in the present? Would she really enjoy these simple occupations, if she had to do them all day, forever? The works surveyed restage the Hesiodic vision of a humankind that remains itself through a succession of local forms as a choice for the most satisfying capabilities of the human animal. Their literal-minded realism manifests the seriousness with which they mean the reader to decide about the forms of life they portray. In the introduction to *Full Circle*, for example, John Collier distinguishes the stakes of this realist project as a commitment to envisioning a possible future in all the details of its livability, quite apart from the question of how such a future might come about:

> Having imagined this state of affairs, it has been my business to describe it closely just as I would a Malayan settlement or a

neolithic meal or ceremony, but not to *account* for it merely because it happens to take place in the future. I believe that, given a certain impetus, things may take this sort of course and in as short a time, despite the obvious objections, but I am not concerned to document a tale with all the artistic untruths of why and wherefore.[14]

Postapocalyptic fictions invite the reader to commit to a future that she can only reach if she detaches herself from present forms of care. Fictions that stage the return of historical forms of life typically imagine them as a repository of latent goods that have been lost or forgotten in the present. By contrast, in Cormac McCarthy's *The Road* (2006), Jim Crace's *The Pesthouse* (2007), and Emily St. John Mandel's *Station Eleven* (2014), the past has no such value. In these novels, the past does not appear as a particular form of life, holistically imagined in its potential for the recovery of human capabilities, but as a disaggregated array of motifs that threaten survival efforts with the temptations of a world that is gone. Chief among these dangers is the road along which the postapocalyptic survivors must travel. It represents the inability to survive in the place where one finds oneself and entails unavoidable exposure to the worst that human predation has to offer.

The road too is an ancient motif. In Hesiod's vision of organized human life successively destroyed by the enmity of the gods, it is an image of survivalism at its harshest, the place where a poorly made wagon will break its axle, spilling survival goods to the ground, and exposing its owner to robbery, mockery, and starvation. Hesiod's precarious transport is the distant ancestor of the handcarts and shopping trolleys to which the protagonists of postapocalyptic fiction entrust their futures, as they try to shepherd what little remains to them from point A to point B. His road as site of deadly exposure has a large set of modern avatars, from

14. Collier (1933) vi.

the Watling Street of Edward Shanks's *The People of the Ruins* (1920), to the cracked, collapsed, and treacherous freeways of Octavia Butler's *Parable of the Sower* (1993) and Cormac McCarthy's *The Road* (2006). The road is a marker of authorial dubiousness with regard to the expanded set of capabilities afforded to characters in postapocalyptic fictions that showcase the return of the past.

Survivalism as such is mostly an unhappy sidebar in the history of postapocalyptic fiction—a salutary reminder of how badly things can go wrong when you try to go it alone. David Brin's *The Postman* (1985) memorializes the "armed and armored hermits" whose hobby was "thinking about the fall of society and fantasizing about what they would do after it happened," but who, when their moment arrives, are soon picked off by better-armed, more organized groups of raiders.[15] Likewise, in Octavia Butler's *Parable* novels, "armed and armored" survivalists who seek salvation in seclusion and firepower eventually lose out to communitarian endeavors.

Posthuman survivalist fiction is a special category, however. Richard Matheson's *I Am Legend* (1954) and Colson Whitehead's *Zone One* (2011) take the war of the single, male, heavily armed, human survivor against a swarm of posthumans as their basic scenario. The simple occupation in these fictions is killing, and they reverse the relationship between occupation and mentation in postapocalyptic fiction more generally. Rather than allowing new forms of mental life to emerge automatically from new practices of daily life, the survivor must struggle to overcome persistent forms of mentation that will otherwise destroy him. The hero of *I Am Legend* must resist his urge to "be one" with the vampires that surround him, and this resistance requires him to do the ontological work of separating himself from what appears to be alive in the world around him but is not truly living in the way that he himself is alive. So, too, the protagonist of *Zone One* must engage in

---

15. Brin (1985) 44, 276.

frequent ontological fitness tests if he is to remain alert to the continuous zombie creep into his lifeworld.

The deep model for these fictions is Henry David Thoreau's *Walden* (1854). Nathaniel Hawthorne analyzes its practices of ontological distantiation—its author's painstaking categorization of life-forms into what is more or less alive in comparison with himself—in his last romance, *Septimius Felton, or the Elixir of Life* (1872), which is based on a story told to him by Thoreau, and tells of a lonely survivalist holed up in the vicinity of Walden Pond, working out how to get more life for himself by separating himself from other living beings.

In chapter 3, then, "Survivalist Anthropology," I look at postapocalyptic fiction that brackets the direct, immediately productive relationship between occupation and mentation, and posits instead the need for constant ontological practice as a prerequisite of survival. Whereas this practice is an adversarial strategy in posthuman survivalist fiction, in Octavia Butler's *Parable* novels (1993–98), the Earthseed writings of her protagonist, Lauren Oya Olamina, sustain eucharistic functions of community creation and group adhesion in a world whose defining characteristic is instability. Communal rehearsal of Earthseed's ontological claims is a requirement for admission to the survivor group, on the understanding that human beings' relationships with one another are directly commensurate with their relationships to other living beings and the lifeworld as a whole. Having the version of this relationship that they need to survive will not come about automatically through a return to simple occupations but is a capability they must foster through ontological practice. Butler's figure of the Sower fulfills the organic meaning of *apokalypsis*. If a new form of life is to take root, the survivor group must become the fallow ground in which its characteristic forms of mentation can establish themselves and its potential unfold. Butler restages the Hesiodic vision of a humankind that remains itself through a succession of local forms as a question about succession and submission. Would the reader be willing to serve as the receptacle for another's vision, to be the seedbed of a future she will not and cannot know?

For Hesiod, Mary Shelley, and Olaf Stapledon, the articulation of humanness that emerges from their reflections on the relationship between occupation and mentation is an author-level function that gives them their authority as didactic figures positioned at a higher level of understanding than their readers and characters. For the authors I look at in chapter 2, such articulations of humanness are best avoided. Insofar as their characters have emerged into new forms of mental life through their new occupations, they enact a version of humankind whose interiority is inaccessible to the author who can only observe their happiness from the outside, even when it recapitulates a historical form of life on the same terrain they themselves inhabit. In the case of the authors I examine in chapter 3, the articulation of humanness in relation to other life-forms and the lifeworld as a whole is pushed down onto their characters. While we may understand these characters as mouthpieces for authorial ideas, in the world of their fictions their ability to articulate what it is to be human, either to themselves or to others, is a distinctive form of survivalism. It is a capability that means they survive better than those who try to get by without their careful ontological reflection upon, and discrimination between, the life-forms they encounter. Survival brings prestige, and prestige brings followers, so that further real and symbolic capital accrues to their practice.

What all these kinds of postapocalyptic fiction have in common, however, is a commitment to staging human beings living on after catastrophe, and to showing why catastrophe is necessary for the new forms of human sociality they envision. The contrast between Jean-Baptiste Cousin de Grainville's *Le dernier homme* (1805) and Mary Shelley's *The Last Man* highlights the difference between apocalyptic and postapocalyptic fiction in this regard. Grainville's novel is set in the distant future and focuses on the last couple as they worry over whether an empty world should be repopulated or not. Eschatological ethics are different from survival ethics. They do not include the recovery of occluded capabilities, the relationship between occupation and mentation, or the ways in which these might offer a foundation for new forms of social life.

For this reason, I have omitted from detailed consideration works of last-man fiction other than *The Last Man* itself, since these too are mostly focused on the apocalyptic event, rather than what comes after it, as well as apocalyptic fictions that are more interested in the psychology of loss than the prospects for living on, such as Denis Johnson's *Fiskadoro*, Doris Lessing's *The Memoirs of a Survivor*, and David Markson's *Wittgenstein's Mistress*. I mention these only in passing in relation to the realist project that postapocalyptic fiction commits itself to in its undertaking to stage life after the end in its daily details. Likewise, I do not consider dystopias of the near future, such as Chang-Rae Lee's *On Such a Full Sea* and Edan Lepucki's *California*, or the satirical variety of postapocalyptic fiction represented by Walter M. Miller's *A Canticle for Leibowitz*, Will Self's *The Book of Dave*, and Emily St. John Mandel's *Station Eleven*, in which a randomly surviving document determines the form of life for the survivors of the apocalyptic event. In short, I omit fictions that do not commit themselves to imagining a postapocalyptic future in which human beings live better than they do now.

Of the several book-length studies of postapocalyptic fiction that have appeared in recent years, Claire Curtis's *Postapocalyptic Fiction and the Social Contract* is most closely akin to my own concerns. For Curtis, "thinking the end of the world" is a way of imagining the forms of social organization in which starting over might happen. Curtis pairs social theorists with fiction writers in each chapter, and I share her understanding that postapocalyptic fiction affords a "spatial and bodily context" for the primitivism of state-of-nature theorists.[16] Mary Manjikian's *Apocalypse and Post-Politics*

---

16. Curtis (2010) 2–4. As I make clear in chapter 2, I do not share her understanding of the lack of detail in Rousseau's presentation of indigenous life.

likewise explains the recent spike in postapocalyptic fiction in large-scale social theoretical terms and is especially concerned with the ways in which its post-state scenarios imagine forms of direct, risky, face-to-face care that have been eclipsed or supplanted by the surrogate agency of the modern bureaucratic state.[17]

I have also benefited from the historical perspective of Teresa Heffernan's *Post-Apocalyptic Culture*, in which postapocalyptic fiction is understood to enact a renunciation of the task of a rational unveiling of human perfectibility, as this task is entailed in the "slide from religion to philosophy" in post-Kantian philosophy. My own concern to show how mentation is imagined to proceed directly from occupation in such fiction is continuous with Heffernan's understanding of a postapocalyptic subject that cannot realize its capabilities through rational projection of goals and satisfactions, although my readings keep to a more narrowly delimited archive than hers. In chapter 3, I discuss the use of the term "postapocalyptic" to refer to American Indian novels of reservation life, but elsewhere it refers to unintended catastrophes, rather than to a present that does not yet understand itself as such, as the term is used in James Berger's *After the End*, with which Heffernan's usage is convergent.[18] I signal my indebtedness to the many excellent readings in Heather Hicks's *The Post-Apocalyptic Novel in the Twenty-First Century* and John Hay's *Postapocalyptic Fantasies in Antebellum American Literature* in my discussions of particular works that they also treat.

The most cogent study of postapocalyptic fiction for the goals of this project is, however, Warren Wagar's *Terminal Visions: The Literature of Last Things*. Wagar's survey of the apocalyptic and postapocalyptic varietals of speculative fiction is both exhaustive

---

17. Manjikian (2012) 28–29, 294–302 invokes Donna Haraway's concept of "vision" through fiction, and Levinas's contrast between "face-to-face" proximity to the neighbor and "side-by-side" proximity in the bureaucratic state.

18. Heffernan (2008) 4–7.

and continuously illuminating, and my emphasis on the themes of occupation, ontology, and the anthropological horizon is intended to flesh out the positive characteristics of postapocalyptic life that he sketches so suggestively in his overview of the archive as a whole.[19] The claim I make throughout is that while critical readings of postapocalyptic fiction have rightly identified its commitment to starting over, they have generally mischaracterized it by beginning at the macrosocial level, with the social contract and other large-scale forms of social organization, rather than the single human being and their body.

Fictions that stage projects of solo regeneration beyond the confines of organized society might seem at first sight like whimsical or irresponsible reflections on human potential by the very fact that they imagine such regeneration to be possible without the supports of organized society. What I suggest, however, is that postapocalyptic fiction advances a strand of political thought that is as ancient as Aristotle's student Dicaearchus, who argued, against his teacher, that the polis is not the best form of life for the realization of human potential. Indeed, ideas about human potential are necessarily mistaken if their horizon is limited to the polis, since human beings are not able to exercise there the capabilities that bring them genuine satisfaction. We should look elsewhere— to poetic fictions, and their memories of prior forms of life—to understand what human beings are capable of and how it is best for them to live.

Postapocalyptic fiction's visions of regeneration beyond the polis walls can therefore be understood as prosocial experiments. They stage new forms of sociality that might emerge if the body and its capabilities were properly appreciated as the measure by which to gauge the degree to which human beings are likely to be contented with the form of social life they belong to. Its protagonists must exit the polis to discover these capabilities, and social life must therefore be reimagined from the outside in. Outsider

19. Wagar (1982) 71–74.

knowledge is a prerequisite for a new vision of what living together might look like.

Capabilities theory is a helpful window into what is at stake here. As pioneered by Amartya Sen and Martha Nussbaum, capabilities theory seeks to give political impetus to what is best for human beings to be doing for themselves in the present without relying on metrics like GDP and GNP that measure macrosocial achievements without regard for their impact on actual human beings. It is a person-centric approach to well-being and is similarly skeptical of aggregating philosophical approaches to human happiness such as utilitarianism that sink the experiences of the individual in an arithmetical common good. Instead, it takes a bottom-up approach. Its fundamental question is "What are people actually able to do and to be?" And it poses this question to actual living people—how do they want to live, and what opportunities to develop their capabilities can they realistically be afforded by their governments?[20]

Capabilities activism means to advance political change without recourse to ideal theory—to give people the chance to become what they themselves would choose to be. But its commitment to being an engine of real-world change makes it vulnerable to a Rousseauian critique of the capabilities it means to foster. In its weak form, such a critique would consist simply in pointing out gaps and blind spots in its range. Presentism, for example, is virtually unavoidable if the capabilities to be fostered are drawn from those available in the here and now. The strong form of the critique would be that a misunderstanding of capabilities is not simply a matter of gaps and blind spots that could be corrected by shared investigative efforts aimed at producing a more comprehensive list. According to the strong form of the critique, any such

---

20. See Nussbaum (2011) 33–34 for a list of ten core capabilities that all governments should seek to enhance for their citizens: life; bodily health; bodily integrity; senses, imagination, and thought; emotions; practical reason; affiliation; other species; play; control over one's environment.

attempt is bound to fail, not through oversight and omission, but because the understanding of what capabilities are on the part of the inquirers and their subjects is limited by the form of social life within which the inquiry is conducted. Both inquirers and subjects are incapable of knowing what is good for them or what they are capable of, because they have never seen better examples of human capability than the human beings they encounter in the world they belong to.

This form of the critique is advanced by Rousseau in *The Discourse on Inequality*. The best that the subjects of modernity can hope for is to try to relearn what they are capable of, and what would make them truly happy, by acquainting themselves with the free peoples of the earth. It is within this horizon that postapocalyptic fiction pursues its investigations. It imagines a world in which the normative demands of the present have become inoperable. There is no more capitalism and no more nation-state. As basic survival skills are relearned, there is typically a return to earlier forms of sociality, often those that indigenous people adopted on the same terrain. New capabilities are enabled by the apocalyptic event, and these capabilities bring new satisfactions that could not have been anticipated in the world that is gone. This is a point that postapocalyptic fiction makes time and time again. Human beings could not have helped themselves to a better future. They can only arrive in it through a kind of secular providence. What they thought they wanted was a mistake, and only with the destruction of what they made for themselves can they begin again, disentangling themselves from old ways of thinking and their misconceptions of human happiness.

It is by bringing capabilities theory into dialogue with speculative anthropology that we can best understand the historical horizon of postapocalyptic fiction, and the vision of human regeneration it is meant to subtend and advance.[21] Assent to polis culture

---

21. Csicsery-Ronay (2008) 34–36, 105–108 likewise notes the importance of revisionary cultural anthropology for the "retrofutures" of science fiction since the 1960s.

persists because of its promise that daily life can be made painless and secure. This insulation from harm comes at a high cost—the loss of the body's capabilities and the individual's ability to choose her commitments for herself. Postapocalyptic fiction allows its readers to work forward from the individual person's experience of what they are capable of, to forms of shared life in which these capabilities are not abrogated in the life of the whole—forms of shared life that impress its protagonists as meaningful, lasting, worthwhile extensions of relationality, because they originate in the need or desire or will to share, in contrast to their previous experience of finding themselves immersed in a mass of social relations they did not choose, could not remake, and could never leave: the compulsory entanglement of modernity.

Any such step-by-step, volitional extension of relationality can only be a fiction for the readers of postapocalyptic fiction, and insofar as postapocalyptic fiction asserts that the imaginative possibilities it presents cannot be realized through political struggle or critical engagement with present forms of life, it stands in a different relationship to the possibilities it stages than other kinds of speculative fiction—outside the cautionary mode of dystopian imaginings of the near future that seek to prevent the possibilities they imagine, or of utopian visions that seek to advance their own realization.

If this is the case, then how can postapocalyptic fiction be anything other than the kind of pernicious distraction that "apocaholism" names? Darko Suvin observes that in its frequent staging of worlds "without money-economy, state apparatus, and depersonalizing urbanization," science fiction is closer to pastoral poetry than it is to fantasy literature. But pastoral is to science fiction as alchemy is to chemistry and nuclear physics: "An early try in the right direction with insufficient foundations." Pastoral was naïve because its experiments in social engineering were pitched at the level of the individual. It believed it could usefully engage with ideas of human freedom by staging individual lives outside the polis walls, yet without the macrosocial structures the polis instantiates, any such freedoms can only be daydreams that contribute to political quietism: "Men are the historical destiny of man; the synthesis in this triad is a *humanistic collectivism*."[22]

Suvin's understanding that it is only meaningful to imagine human freedom within the form of a possible collective, because it is only within a collective that freedom can emerge, as an excess to natural need and dependence, is consistent with the political ontology of Marx and Aristotle, for whom the polis is ontologically prior to the singular human being: a human being as such is only possible in the polis, because it is only there that the potential to be a human being can be realized. The truly human life that comes into being with the civilization of the polis is in excess of and in opposition to the natural life of need-based occupations. In antiquity, this view was most strongly associated with Aristotle in his *Politics*, while his pupil Dicaearchus, in his *Life of Greece*, argued in terms similar to Rousseau that thinking about what human beings are capable of with only the examples of the polis before your eyes will inevitably produce a false view of human possibility. It is instead to poetry—and especially to poetry that imagines the Golden Age—that we should look, if we want an imaginative understanding of what real freedom might look like.

Suvin's analogy between speculative fiction and pastoral is therefore better than he realizes, and it holds true with special force in the case of postapocalyptic fiction. Both pastoral and postapocalyptic fiction set themselves against the idea that a change for the better in human social relations can proceed directly from a vision of the collective. They are prosocial on the understanding that any new collective must be grounded in an individual, body-centric recovery of capabilities that can only emerge outside the polis walls. The world-building of postapocalyptic fiction is geared toward the production of narratives in which its protagonists can leave the polis behind and contrast the freedoms and capabilities they discover outside it with those they

---

22. Suvin (1979) 8–9, 75.

knew before. Its classic structure is a before-and-after story in which the characters, and vicariously the reader, experience the worlds of before and after in such a way that they can choose between them—the apocalypse on trial I have referred to already.

The form of freedom staged in pastoral and postapocalyptic fiction—the individual's recovery of powers and capabilities outside the polis walls—is marronage. The term originates in colonial discourse. The maroon is a plantation slave who has escaped bondage, sometimes with the hope of joining a group of fugitives beyond the reach of plantation life. The word derives from the Spanish *cimarrón*, a de-domesticated animal that escaped confinement and fled to the hills. In his classic study of maroon societies in the Caribbean and the eastern seaboard of the Americas, Richard Price notes the derivation of the idea of freedom instantiated in these societies from animal life, and the subsequent clustering around it of related ideas of wildness, fierceness, and unbrokenness.[23]

Maroon societies instantiate a form of life in which an individual's recovery of freedom and capabilities outside the polis walls precedes their reintegration into a collective, and their capacity to model a new form of social life for those left behind. Marronage subtends the invention of pastoral as a literary form in Greco-Roman antiquity. In the ancient Mediterranean, Sicily was

---

23. Price (1979) 1–2 n.1. For its continuing importance to Edouard Glissant and Caribbean political theory more generally, see Wynter (1989). The equivalent Greek term ἀτιμαγέλης occurs twice in the corpus of pastoral fiction attributed to Theocritus, where it characterizes animals who refuse to participate in herding behavior, and is explained as "herd shunning" in Aristotle's *History of Animals* 572b19, 611a8: it is especially common for uncastrated bulls to engage in this behavior at mating time, but they may do so at other times too, and thereby run the risk of destruction from predators in the wild. The maroon as rogue male informs the comparison of Oedipus to a wild bull in *Oedipus the King* 477–78, and the scholiast to Pindar who notes that Amphitryon sees the temper and disposition of his half-human adoptive son Heracles as tending outside human law (ἐκνόμιον: *Nemean* 1.56–58).

the major center of plantation agriculture, and it was also the birthplace of pastoral fiction in the work of the Greek poet Theocritus, who was born and raised in the Greek-speaking Sicilian city of Syracuse. On Sicily's plantations, there were two kinds of slave: field slaves bound to their estate, and herdsman slaves who worked off site, under the supervision of a "herd master." Herdsman slaves had to be armed to perform their duties, which included defending the herds against wild animals and rustlers, and they also had to be at liberty to follow the herds. Sometimes these armed herdsmen did not return to their plantations. Occasionally they were the instigators of full-scale slave revolts, but more frequently they just slipped away to form maroon communities in Sicily's backcountry.[24]

The poetry of Theocritus stands at the head of a long history of reflection on the relationship between human and animal freedom, and human and animal silence, in the pastoral genre. The understanding that human beings can relearn what it is to be free from the behavior of domesticated animals is a feature of the pastoral tradition emphasized in the early modern reception of Virgil's *Eclogues* in England. An early seventeenth-century commentary on the idea of *libertas* in eclogue 1 observes:

> My freedome &c. A specious tittle, and a very reasonable pretext, and such as might easily pierse the simple mind of a Shepheard; *it being even imprinted in the disposition of all creatures as well reasonable, as others, naturally to affect freedome: which principle is found most true by daily experience, in such birds, and beasts, as by mans art are reclaimed, how loath they are to yeeld unto bondage; and being subdued, if never so little left to themselves,*

---

24. Shaw (2001) 11, 51–68. Cf. Csicsery-Ronay (2003) 238: "Even the classical genres to which sf is often traced (the pastoral, the romance, the utopian cityscape) originate in the imperial imagination (specifically from Alexandria, Byzantium, and Rome), as do their shadow-genres, the slave's narrative, the journey through hell, and the dark city."

how soone they apprehend their first estate and freedome, and how warily they preserve themselves from being enthralled againe.

Annabel Patterson notes that the italicized passage is not to be found in the work of Juan Luis Vives that forms the basis of the scholarly portions of this commentary on the *Eclogues* by "W. L."[25] Rather, the expansive gloss develops an idea that is common in the poetic reception of the *Eclogues* and which sustains the vitality of pastoral in the nineteenth century as a site for thinking about the relationship between human political freedom and the freedoms of nonhuman life.

John Clare is the nineteenth century's great poet of natural freedom, but his poems offer a more precarious iteration of its affordances for human emulation than Theocritus's *Idylls* or Virgil's *Eclogues*. Because of the devastation of local nonhuman worlds in his time, especially the drastic curtailment of the freedoms of nonhuman life produced by enclosure, free natural beings can increasingly only be found in poems, and not on the relics of their own terrain, where they were once encountered: "The poet's song will be | The only refuge they can find."[26] Just as for Dicaearchus, poetry becomes vitally important for the future of human life because it is a site where natural freedom is remembered and preserved.

Clare is insistent that the occupation of shepherd let him "keep [his] spirit with the free," because it let him be where "nature seems to have her own sweet will." He claims time and again that he learned his ethical and poetic freedom from Nature. The "leafhid forest and lonely shore | Seem to my mind like beings that are

25. The commentary has been attributed to William Latham and William L'Isle. Patterson (1987) 167–68 attributes it to Latham, Munro (2013) 50 to L'Isle, a scholar of Anglo-Saxon: "L'Isle naturalizes Virgil as an indigenous poet, transforming his predecessor's plants and flowers into their English equivalents." Curran (1986) 106 observes that indigeneity as freedom from alien governance fuels the popularity of pastoral in nineteenth-century colonial contexts, although it is not obvious that L'Isle intends more than to resituate the generic possibilities of pastoral in the British Isles and its vernaculars, continuing the work of Spenser in this regard.

26. Clare (2003) 88.

free," and being with them leaves "the mind as its creator free."[27] The encounter with what comes into being out of its own generativity allows him to understand what in himself and his work is truly his own, and what is an imposition of human contrivance. Likewise, he insists, pastoral is the genre that makes this experience of freedom available and apprehensible to others:

> Rurallity I dearly love thee
> Simple as thy numbers run
> Epics song may soar above thee
> Still thy sweetness yields to none
> Cots to sing and woods and vales
> Tho its all thy reed can do
> These with nature shall prevail
> When epics war harps broke in two[28]

The natural freedom that Clare learns from nonhuman life must of necessity be enacted by him as stolen freedom—the moments of respite from the imposition of labor that are common to the herdsman and the domesticated animal alike. As *The Shepherd's Calendar* makes clear, he views this understanding of freedom as one of the essential cognitive affordances of the pastoral tradition that he is continuing in his own poetic work:

> The gladden'd swine bolt from the sty
>   And round the yard in freedom run,
> Or stretching in their slumber lie
>   Beside the cottage in the sun.
> The young horse whinneys to his mate,
>   And, sickening from the thresher's door,
> Rubs at the straw-yard's banded gate
>   Longing for freedom on the moor.[29]

---

27. Clare (2003) 274, 241–43.
28. Clare (2004) 59.
29. Clare (2006) 49.

In addition to Clare's meditations on selfhood under enclosure, Thomas Chatterton's *African Eclogues*, Robert Southey's *Botany Bay Eclogues*, and Edward Rushton's *West Indian Eclogues* continue to find inspiration for human freedom in the figuration of nonhuman life in the pastoral tradition.[30] The freedom of nonhuman life is a necessary detour, a discovery of potential forms of human selfhood in the nonhuman other, by means of which human beings can be awoken to the impoverishment of their inner experience in the absence of political freedom, and galvanized toward its recovery.

In his documentary presentation of evidence relating to ancient marronage, Roman social historian Brent Shaw cites the legal compendium known as the *Digest* on the nature of fugitive freedom: "Flight is a type of liberty, in that the slave has escaped from his master's power, even if only for the moment."[31] Freedom is actualized in escape, however brief the experience. Fugitivity canalizes a natural movement toward the outside, and there must therefore be an outside toward which this impetus can be directed.

Recent political theory has likewise emphasized unowned space as a necessary condition for the enactment of the idea of freedom operative in marronage. Marronage is a pursuit of freedom grounded in the nature of the human animal and its will to be free, just as it is in the nonhuman animal that seizes its opportunity to break free from confinement. What we should understand here, Jimmy Casas Klausen argues, is the emergence of a drive that takes Nature as the necessary horizon of freedom. This drive does not represent Nature to itself mythically or nostalgically, as the site of an authentic past or a place of origins. Rather, it "deploys nature poetically as a concept of potential freedom that tactically contests the hegemony of political modernity's domination."[32]

---

30. Curran (1986) 85–127.
31. Shaw (2001) 52.
32. Klausen (2014) 226–28.

This is a fairly bare form of accounting for experience, as is proper to theory, but we can supplement its experiential content with the imagining of the moment in which fugitivity emerges in Patrick Chamoiseau's *Slave Old Man*. This moment is rapturous, bewildering, a violent cancellation of the inner life of the slave that is hardly comprehensible at first even to its own subject. It is a "combustion," a convulsive event, in which "every object in his cabin sweats blood all ablaze, and the polished earth underfoot takes fire as well." But it is also the moment in which the natural world regains its sanctity. The forest shows itself anew as "the cavern of ages," a pristine site in which "no one seems ever to have trod": "The impression of entering a sanctuary becomes intoxicating; an untold authority asserts itself over the darkness within which (and with which) he runs."[33]

We have grown suspicious of pristine Nature and its authority, but Neil Roberts reminds us that Nature, as a space in which to enact the natural freedom reflected back to human beings by nonhuman lives, was a vital inspiration for New World fugitives.[34] In *My Bondage and My Freedom*, for example, Frederick Douglass spotlights the critical agency of Nature at the decisive moment of escape: "I am in the wood, buried in its somber gloom, and hushed in its solemn silence; hid from all human eyes; shut in with nature and nature's God, and absent from all human contrivances." An understanding of the decisiveness of Nature's presence at this critical juncture remains with Douglass in his maturity as he continues to reflect on the fact that, for the slave, "civilization is shut out, but nature cannot be." He emphasizes the importance of the slave child's opportunity to abide with nonhuman lives for his experience of freedom, in contrast to the confined existence of white

---

33. Chamoiseau (2018) 36, 51–52; cf. 80–81 on the "Great Woods that knew the Before, that harbored the communion host of an innocence gone by, and which trembled with primal forces," where "escapees looked upon the trees as if contemplating a cathedral."

34. Roberts (2015) 51–138.

youths. The slave-boy is "a genuine boy," doing "whatever his boyish nature suggests," with these suggestions coming in large part from the animals he lives with. As he emulates "all the strange antics and freaks of horses, dogs, pigs, and barn-door fowls," he "literally runs wild," enacting an understanding of freedom for himself in the exercise of his own body.[35] In these moments, the slave-boy practices freedom, while white children can only think about it.

So, too, in *Blake*, Martin Delany, whatever his points of dispute with Douglass, agrees with him in finding in the natural world the impetus and example for slaves' insurrection: "So simple is it that the trees of the forest or an orchard illustrate it; flocks of birds or domestic cattle, fields of corn hemp or sugar cane; tobacco rice or cotton, the whistling of the wind, rustling of the leaves, flashing of lightning, roaring of thunder, and running of streams all keep it constantly before their eyes and in their memory, so that they cannot forget it if they would."[36] In his sonnet "To Toussaint L'Ouverture," Wordsworth claims that the identity between the freedom of natural motion and the human will to political freedom has been made forever legible and unforgettable in the form of his revolutionary life, reverting to pastoral's long history of reflection on the inspiration to human freedom discoverable in nonhuman agency:

> Thou hast left behind
> Powers that will work for thee; air, earth, and skies.
> There's not a breathing of the common wind
> That will forget thee.[37]

---

35. Douglass (2003) 172, 50, 35.
36. Delany (2017) 40–41.
37. Thomas (2000) 109–10 reads Wordsworth's sonnet as an example of the "appropriation and concealment of abolitionist discourse contained within Romantic poetry." I would instead suggest that it articulates a common ground with this discourse in their shared understanding of the inspirational agency of nonhuman life.

Douglass discovers the will to be free in nonhuman lives and allows it to inspire him to action. In the maroon episode of *Blake*, "Henry at Large," Delany's protagonist voyages away from the eastern seaboard, crossing the Red River, the Yazoo, and the Ouachita. Here, in the "wilderness" of the trans-Mississippi, for the first time since his maturity into manhood, "responsibilities rose up in a shape of which he had no conception." Dread comes over him, as "dangers stood staring him in the face at every step he took," but he is able to map this encounter with the American wilderness onto the biblical space of Moses in the desert.

Blake's journey is a venture beyond the polis that gives shape and purpose to future aspirations. These could not be envisaged without the experience of learning to survive in an outer space in which responsibilities—and capabilities—begin.[38] When he later visits the "bold, courageous, and fearless adventurers, denizens of the mystical, antiquated, and almost fabulous Dismal Swamp," this earlier generation of famous maroons "hailed the daring runaway as the harbinger of better days." Like them, he has acquired a range of survival skills in order to overcome what Jerome McGann, in his commentary, calls the "series of practical tests that the fugitives confront," and this experience provides the groundwork for a society to come.[39]

So, too, a century later, Aimé Césaire will enjoin his compatriots to lay hold of the experience of the Caribbean's native forest and remember the part it played in their recovery of freedom.[40] Edouard Glissant likewise emphasizes poetry's role in freeing up the landscape as an imaginative space that offers vital affordances

---

38. Delany (2017) 70–71.

39. Delany (2017) 113, 132–33. The text here includes the star map with which Blake and his companions navigate their way through the woods by night as an example of the practical skills they acquire in the wilderness. The printed version is a copy of Delany's original drawing, which has not survived, "a beautiful diagram of Ursa Major, or the Great Bear, drawn by the author—called Henry's Plan of the North Star, drawn on a stump in a forest of Louisiana." See Delany (2017) 324 n.122.

40. Roberts (2015) 6–7.

for political freedom: "When space is beyond our control, when we are not able to frequent it freely, when, between the self and the landscape, there is an extensive series of barriers, those engendered by dispossession and exploitation, the relationship to landscape is clearly constrained and strangled. Consequently, to free the relationship to landscape through a poetic act, through poetic speech, is an act of freedom."[41] Pastoral keeps marronage in mind.

Nature is what the maroon must have in order to be free. But on an earth that no longer offers unowned spaces, like the hills of Sicily and the New World that beckoned to the maroon, apocalyptic events assume the role of clearing the ground of its owners and making such spaces available again. Postapocalyptic fiction is the pastoral of our time. It posits a space of freedom that a would-be subject of freedom can access in order to enact their emergence as free. This emergence into freedom proves to be prosocial, but the first step is a step toward the outside. The individualism and small-scale sociality of postapocalyptic fiction are not naïve. They are the necessary ground for choosing the freedoms and capabilities we would want to see preserved in any future collective that might emerge from them.

Nature as a space for the emergence of human capabilities and freedoms is fundamental to the world-building of postapocalyptic fiction. The chapters of this book are a tour of the forms they take there: what they look like, where they come from, what the operative conditions are for their emergence, and what might prevent their prosocial endeavors from taking root in the long term. We have already met some of the figures that inhabit this space: Rousseau's indigene, the New World maroon, Octavia Butler's Sower. On the way we will meet others, and in the conclusion, "Landscape with Figures," I investigate the ontology of the figure itself. What is this being poised between fiction, theory, and historical existence, and what affordances for thinking does it offer? What

---

41. Glissant, in Obrist and Raza (2017) 94.

does it mean to think with a figure in the landscapes of postapocalyptic fiction?

I ask these questions of two figures of freedom from mid-twentieth-century political theory, Ernst Jünger's forest fleer and Carl Schmitt's cosmopartisan, in order to better understand the ways in which the figure is essential to staging the emergence of freedom from disaster. Theorizing a moment at which the modern state seemed on the verge of maximal penetration into the life of its subjects and of eliminating any outside to itself, Jünger and Schmitt ask themselves whether we must "count on catastrophe" to avoid the absolute and irretrievable installation of global modernity.[42] Has apocalypse become an inevitable horizon for the conception of freedom?

These reflections on catastrophe are convergent with Claude Lévi-Strauss's contemporary admonition in *Tristes tropiques* that the disappearance of the anthropological horizon of the New World has forever removed the possibility of rethinking the idea of freedom in the West. For Lévi-Strauss, it is Rousseau who best understood what was at stake in this lost opportunity. In the superior capabilities of the inhabitants of the New World, Rousseau saw everything that Europeans were incapable of in their hypertrophic forms of social organization reflected back to them as losses—powers for the living of a genuinely happy life they had surrendered, and then forgotten they ever had: "The more I consider these problems, the more I am convinced that they admit of no reply other than the one given by Rousseau: . . . It was he who taught us that, after demolishing all forms of social organization, we can still discover the principles which will allow us to construct a new form."[43]

That demolition is required to start over, Jünger, Schmitt, and Lévi-Strauss agree. What I suggest in the conclusion is that the figure, as a way of imagining the demolition and the starting over,

---

42. Jünger (2013) 43.
43. Lévi-Strauss (1992) 390–93.

is a foretaste of the freedoms it imagines. The maroon, the forest fleer, and the cosmopartisan are neither real nor imaginary, historical or fictional. Neither are the Trickster, the Sower, the Indian, and the Stone Age Hunter, all of whom we shall encounter in due course. The figure begins the work of stepping toward the outside by being itself an instance of free imaginative regeneration. It draws upon history without being confined by historical details, and its inventors must maintain their exteriority toward a form of life whose inner world they can only guess at. In contrast to the steady creep of modernity's intrusions, the figure instantiates a freedom to come by keeping its distance from us. The appeal to the figure is an appeal to what cannot be known.

1

The Apocalyptic Cosmos

MARY SHELLEY'S *The Last Man* is a curious case for genre studies. Part plague chronicle, part *roman-à-clef*, part future history, it is also the first work in a mode of speculative fiction it played no part in founding. Appearing at a moment when Romantic enthusiasm for apocalyptic fantasies was largely played out, it was derided at the time of its publication in 1826 and remained little known until its 1965 U.S. reprint, by which time last man narratives and post-apocalyptic tales of various kinds were a staple of speculative fiction. *The Last Man* thus precedes the circumscription of post-apocalyptic fiction as genre writing. It does not offer itself as storytelling in a minor key or in the marginal voice of an unheeded prophet. The models it presents for its project are major: Greek epic and Hesiod, in particular. Its story of humankind destroyed by a plague that leaves the rest of life unharmed looks to Greek antecedents for its vision of human victimization at the hands of a whimsical cosmos. In Hesiod, Shelley found not only thematic precedents but a model for the scale of her endeavor: a vision of what it would be like for all of humanity to perish, more or less in one go.[1]

---

1. There was a corpus of end-of-the-world poetry in existence when Shelley published *The Last Man*, a significant portion of which had been written by members of her own circle. For the literary history, see Snyder (1978). The novel's triple-decker format is a massive elaboration of these contemporary suggestions. It takes literary

It is this sense of scale—a global scale appropriate to our present ecological predicament—that Amitav Ghosh has argued is lacking in contemporary realist fiction. The mode of fiction that peaked in the great nineteenth-century realist novels, and whose workings were taken apart, refracted, and remade by the modernists, excels at fine-grained staging of character and action, and the fine-grained appraisal of singular fictional beings these afford to the reader. What it is less good at is showing humankind in general responding to global situations and events, with climate change for Ghosh being the development that most urgently calls for a different kind of fictional response. Contemporary fiction, he argues, is hobbled by experimental structures it adopted in the nineteenth century: the small-scale crucibles of testing, proving, and verifying that it shared with contemporary technological innovation. Not only is their scale similar, but the kinds of verification that can be achieved when working at this scale cultivate unwarranted optimism about our powers of understanding and prognostication. The ways human beings act in the world look knowable if the frameworks within which they are studied are the predictable behaviors of the bourgeois family in its everyday settings and scenarios, but these frameworks are now a way of insulating ourselves from basic unknowns in the planetary situation.

The irony for Ghosh is that the forms of realist fiction we now consider normal, and the accumulation of carbon in the earth's atmosphere that renders these forms obsolete, are coeval, Industrial Age, developments. Before this time, human beings everywhere were "catastrophists at heart," with an "instinctive awareness

---

catastrophism from a minor genre of poetic elegy and gives it epic gravity and scale as high-end literary fiction. Given that John Martin was known to Mary Shelley's circle, the scale of her novel may owe something to painterly forms of Romantic apocalypticism; Horn (2014) 62 suggests that the painting-internal observers in Martin's work figure "what only the beholder (or God) is able to see: the destruction of the very instance of observation." Martin's work, in other words, offers a pictorial model for the conflation of authorial and divine perspectives on human victimization in *The Last Man* that I discuss in this chapter.

of the earth's unpredictability."[2] Poetry, in particular, had long had "an intimate relationship with climatic events," but at the very moment when human beings could have used this traditional resource for thinking about their own vulnerability with regard to planetary systems, poetry was superseded as a way of knowing by new technologies of probability in the realist novel. Realist fiction, wittingly or not, served as a booster for human self-confidence, giving its readers an unjustified faith in their ability to forecast their fate and how they would be likely to respond to it.

The outliers in Ghosh's literary history are the various forms of speculative fiction that have maintained the intellectual and cosmic scope which used to be the province of poetry, and epic poetry, in particular. They preserve this scope by treating humankind in the aggregate and rejecting the kinds of singular psychological insights that give the realist novel its precision and prestige.[3] Shelley has a place of honor in this history because her work forcefully rejects the reduction of Nature to setting and ontic frame, which is the process of literary anthropocentrism that the

2. Ghosh (2017) 25–26. As Cooper (2019) observes, citing Hordern and Purcell (2000) 308–309, contemporary archaeology of the Mediterranean world supports Ghosh's argument that the "ecological humility" of early Greek epic reflects the ancient awareness of the precariousness of human survival in fragile ecological conditions: "The interlocking of continuous changes in an inherently unstable environment with the accidental and deliberate effects of human intervention are of the greatest importance in explaining the uncertainties with which human producers have had to cope. But precisely because of the sophistication which those uncertainties have induced on the part of Mediterranean populations, they have not usually caused widespread disaster."

3. Ghosh (2017) 7–27. Lomax (1990) notes the combination of epic scope and "anti-epic" reversal of linear time in *The Last Man*. It is also worth noting that in its commitment to staging generality and ideality under duress, speculative fiction has much in common with the characterology of ancient novels. As Pavel (2013) 23–35 argues, showing how types of human beings respond to such entirely unpredictable and unknowable events as pirate abduction and metamorphosis is preferred to finegrained psychology, and the freedom to stage basic human capabilities in extreme situations was decisive for their early modern appreciation.

nineteenth-century novel accomplishes.[4] Whereas to be modern is to participate in the partitioning of Nature and Culture, and so delimit what the novel can and cannot legitimately treat, Shelley's work is deliberately archaic in its refusal to erect and police this boundary.

Ghosh focuses on *Frankenstein*, but an interventionist Nature is the major agential force in *The Last Man*. It is Nature that, for reasons unknown to human beings, decides to bring humankind to an end, and all the human action in the book is undertaken with respect to this unknowable and unforeseeable apocalyptic event. The effective causes of human annihilation in *The Last Man* are "an unusually warm climate" and a global pestilence, which may or may not be related, and it is when imagining the precariousness of human life with respect to these forces that Shelley has Hesiod especially to hand. She cites (in Elton's translation) *Works and Days* 238–47 on the plagues that Zeus sends to destroy human beings en masse, *Works and Days* 101–105 on the countless harms that wander the earth as silent autonomous agents of Zeus's ill-will toward human beings, and a passage from the fragmentary *Shield of Heracles* 151–53 that describes human bones when the skin has rotted off them and they lie bleaching and crumbling in the sun.[5] These are not passing references but long, inset block quotes, whose frame-breaking function is to direct our attention back to premodern awareness of human precariousness and the literary forms that enshrined this understanding. The series of citations from Hesiod punctuates *The Last Man* with reminders that human beings were not always so confident about their relationship with Nature and that realist fiction did not always look the way it looks now.

Formally, these citations contribute to the staging of *The Last Man* as a weak text. The bulk of the novel's three volumes is a first-person history of the plague written by its last survivor. But this

---

4. Ghosh (2017) 66–73.
5. Shelley (1994) 229, 315, 400.

first-person history is only encountered in the form of Sibylline leaves that the protagonist of the frame narrative discovers by accident in a cave in the course of a tourist visit gone awry. The narrator of the frame narrative transcribes these Sibylline leaves into the first-person history that we read. She tells us she is moved by the story to transcribe it and is also moved in the act of transcribing it, so the text is (fictionally) both contingent and unreliable, for reasons of character, language, and sheer chance, since she might never have found it in the first place. The interruption of the narrative by large, unexplained citations, which may derive from the fictional author, the frame narrator, or Shelley herself, pushes the found manuscript device toward further levels of contingency as a textual assemblage. Its voice from the future is very much a speculative staging, a kind of ghost work.[6]

Tim Morton has noted Shelley's fascination with stories of first contact, anthropology's tales of indigenous others who experience the world in ways quite unlike our own. Frankenstein's Creature experiences a kind of Adamic awakening, a version of the impossible encounter between mature consciousness and the world that is so vividly imagined in book 6 of *Paradise Lost*, but Shelley also sometimes places such moments in her fiction "as a sort of message in the bottle from the future," as in the finder's story of her discovery of the Sibylline leaves in *The Last Man*.[7] Extreme mediation by a weak text is what enables the encounter; fragmentation and distant touching are convergent experiences.

The wonder we encounter in the weak text of *The Last Man* is a single life that has twice experienced the full compass of human cultural possibilities, once as ascent, and a second time as decline. Lionel Verney, the author of the future history recorded in the Sibylline leaves, begins his life in bourgeois prosperity as the son of a royal adviser, but with this adviser's fall from grace he is

---

6. See O'Dea (1992) on the self-conscious textuality of *The Last Man*, and Webb (2000) on the idea of authorship it instantiates.

7. Morton (2003) 264–65.

consigned to the life of a rural shepherd, only to be restored to an advisory role by the son of the ruler his father served. Lionel's life recapitulates the stages of human culture, and his occupation in each of these stages is directly productive of his mentation. After his rescue, just in the nick of time, from pastoral employment, he reflects that "my life was like that of an animal, and my mind was in danger of degenerating into that which informs brute nature"—still a mind, just not a human one. This regression becomes in retrospect a mode of cathexis to the deep past, since in this life he was "as uncouth a savage as the wolf-bred founder of old Rome," a claim that he repeats when he finds himself in Rome, composing his history as the last survivor of the plague.[8]

There are good models for this kind of narrative in Greek literature. In Sophocles' *Philoctetes*, the protagonist is removed from human sociality when he is marooned on Lemnos by the Greek army that is on its way to Troy, and on this island, which Sophocles imagines as uninhabited by human beings, he is integrated into new forms of shared life with other living beings, only to be offered the chance to rejoin history and human culture when Odysseus and his men come back to collect him. The play enacts the crossing of the threshold between early humanity's larger horizon of shared life and the present's more limited forms of human sociality as an event that might occur within a single human life. It stages the farewell look that Nature gives to human beings as subjects of shared life as a glance directed at a singular human being who is leaving this life behind. Callimachus's *Hymn to Demeter* develops this possibility through more severe textual mediation. The tale of the legendary figure Erysichthon, who cuts down a primeval sacred grove and is punished by the goddess Demeter, is told to a contemporary audience by a narrator who seems not to grasp the full import of the story she is telling. Engaging with the form of life in the story involves a

---

8. Cf. Lomax (1990) 8–9 and Canuel (1998) 153–54 on the relationship between primitivism and cultivation in the characterization of Lionel.

similar kind of touching at a distance as the one that is staged in *The Last Man*.⁹

Shelley naturalizes this story type somewhat by stretching it out over an entire developmental autobiography, but it is still legible as such. And Lionel himself signals the convergence of personal and cultural history with a reflection on *Robinson Crusoe*: "The wild and cruel Caribbee, the merciless Cannibal . . . would have been to me a beloved companion . . . his nature would be kin to mine."¹⁰ *Robinson Crusoe* will remain a staple of postapocalyptic fiction, particularly in its survivalist mode, although Crusoe's longing for human companionship will be largely displaced by *Walden's* separatist ontology.¹¹ Here, however, *Crusoe* marks the downhill side of the track that Lionel has previously traced on the way up, from his "degeneration" in the countryside to his rehabilitation as a legitimate human being under the care of Adrian, the son of the king his father advised.

In *The Discourse on Inequality*, Rousseau reflects that what drives such thought experiments in Deep History is the desire to identify the moment in human cultural development at which there was an optimal match between communal resources and

---

9. In Payne (2019), I offer a more extensive account of the role of such weak texts in the primitivism of Hellenistic Greek poetry and its recuperation by Friedrich Schiller in "On Naïve and Sentimental Poetry."

10. Sussman (2003) 294 suggests that in Verney's mind, Crusoe's labor is connected to his ultimate reunion with a larger community, so as to make it appear to him that his own survival work has a similar purpose, whereas *The Last Man* in fact demonstrates "the futility of human labor" in this regard. In what follows, I argue that a relationship between labor and sociality is worked out in the brief period in the novel in which primitive agrarianism brings a social group together and grounds it in shared beliefs, although the life of this survival group is brief. Wang (2011) 244 argues that Verney is an inverted Crusoe, who "reenacts the entire history of capitalist individualism" in reverse, which is true enough, although this reenactment is only one stage in the longer history of humankind that he recapitulates.

11. See Hoberek (2011) 490 and Hicks (2016) 18, 77–78 on the importance of *Crusoe*.

individual capability, so as to note the point at which such development ought to have been arrested:

> There is, I sense, an age at which the individual human being would want to stop; you will look for the age at which you would wish your species had stopped. Discontented with your present state, for reasons that herald even greater discontents for your unhappy posterity, you might perhaps wish to be able to go backwards.[12]

Postapocalyptic fiction is able to translate such unhappy fantasies into fictional realities. Since the author is the one who sets the parameters of cultural regression, she can arrest it at whatever point she wishes and dwell, if only for a short time, on what she believes is the most optimal form of life for human beings, and why. For Shelley, this moment is primitive agriculture, by which she means a form of agricultural production in which all members of the community who consume its goods participate in their production. In this form of life, the relationship between occupation and mentation is the most satisfying to human beings, because it affords them the idea that personal, small-scale, local divinities care about human beings in the same way that human beings care for them.

The return to primitive agriculture is the outcome of the plague's drastic reduction of the human population, and it produces proximity to the ancient Greeks in the form of a return to their mythology. Greek mythology is a natural translation of the lived experience of the survivors. Its return is immediate, not willed or reflective. As the remnant population of Europe goes back to doing the same things all day as the Greeks did, they come to care about the same things as the Greeks did, in much the same way as the Greeks did. Occupation is directly productive of mentation. Because human beings are once again directly dependent on local forms of nonhuman life for their survival, they experience affects of dependency that are directly productive of mythological

---

12. Rousseau (1997) 133.

thought: "Nature with all her changes was invested in divine attributes. The very spirit of the Greek mythology inhabited my heart; I deified the uplands, glades, and streams." This regressive realization of dependency in turn allows for a satire on contemporary forms of knowledge from which such understanding is missing, another persistent theme of postapocalyptic fiction after *The Last Man*.[13]

The change in human life is not one that human beings could have produced for themselves without the apocalyptic event to enable it. William Wagar has observed that postapocalyptic fictions are typically well disposed to the future they imagine. Human life reinvents itself in simpler and more satisfying social forms after the apocalyptic event, and the survivors enjoy what they do all day more than what they did before. The return to the Greeks is what Shelley's version of postapocalyptic positivity looks like, short-lived though it proves to be. In the time that remains, as the trappings of large-scale civilization fall away, her protagonists recover their feeling for the things of the earth along with their "gratitude for the provision for to-morrow's meal." Human dependency and natural providence are realigned, as the blessing that was there all along but only now becomes visible again, when Nature has, whimsically enough, decided to bring humankind to an end. "Our joys were clearer because we saw their end," the survivors reflect.[14] The clarity of purpose that is a common theme of postapocalyptic fiction, now that human action is once again undertaken in the immediate horizon of the life and death of a face-to-face community, is overlaid with the awareness that this recovery of purpose is only possible with the end of days in view. It is what Wagar calls a "terminal vision."[15]

Shelley's engagement with Hesiod is consonant with Ghosh's claim that speculative fiction continues to articulate the cosmic

---

13. Shelley (1994) 308, 431.
14. Shelley (1994) 309, 274.
15. Wagar (1982) 71–74.

pessimism of premodern epic. It is hard to imagine a more committed catastrophist than Hesiod, and Shelley's citations from the poet function both as markers of the scale of her project and of its asymptotic relationship to certainty about the cognitive possibilities it embraces. Her characters have to act in the face of the death of everyone, and in showing their response to a global event that they could in no way have anticipated, she stages the cognitive limitation endemic to Hesiod's world. Cosmic scope and cognitive limitation are the twin constraints of the epic poem, and these twin inheritances converge in *The Last Man*. Humankind as a whole is subject to forms of annihilation it was not able to see coming, and which it could not possibly have seen coming in a cosmos that is not fitted to human intelligibility.

Hesiod is considered the first figure in Western didactic poetry, which is a reasonable label if one bears in mind that his teaching is agnostic on what it is possible and not possible to know, and why. *Works and Days* is didactic poetry without philosophical commitments. It is a text that comes into being before philosophy exists, and it has little in common with the great philosophical epics of antiquity, the poems "About Nature" by Empedocles, Lucretius, and others, in which the world can be known wholly and truly by proceeding from correct philosophical first principles to a rational investigation of its parts.

Hesiod stages human contingency in ways that go far beyond our ordinary understanding of the limits of human sovereignty, autonomy, and agency. Humankind has been annihilated and remade several times already. There is no one reason for the repetitive destruction, and no predictability to it either.[16] Human wrongdoing in the manner of Genesis, the exhaustion of the earth by human overpopulation (the backstory to the Homeric poems), and the gods' dissatisfaction with the creatures they have made, along the lines of the multiple creation stories of the Popol Vuh,

---

16. *Works and Days* 109–201. Lovejoy and Boas (1935) 31 summarize the arbitrariness of the periodic annihilations.

are among the reasons given. The next annihilation will be heralded by the matter of life itself: babies will be born gray-haired as a sign of the apocalypse to come, an indication of imminent renewal that is also found in Diné observations of a "crossover" or "changeover" in traditional forms of life signaling that present ways are nearing their end and a new beginning is at hand.[17]

The gods have no such ill feeling toward other life-forms, which are not subjected to the whimsical malice inflicted on human beings. Humans are the least favored of all living beings, and Hesiod presents himself as the mouthpiece of a humanity that, by definition, consists of postapocalyptic survivors in their entirety, scanning their world for signs of the catastrophe to come with resources that are drastically inferior to those of their divine assailants. Zeus has thirty thousand immortal watchmen who spy on human beings without ever taking a break—a total, infallible, global surveillance network. But lacking the cognitive equipment to recognize impending extinction events is not even the most significant of human impairments. When the gods presented human beings with Pandora as a punishment for their transgressive use of fire, they retro-engineered them so that every single one of them would experience delight in cherishing the instrument of their destruction. Not only do humans not recognize threats, they embrace their own destruction as if it were a good.[18]

The feebleness of human understanding in *Works and Days* makes a strong impression because of the precarious nature of the text itself. Rather than a continuous narrative, like the Homeric epics, the poem consists of advice and opinions on how best to survive in its world that fall into a number of discrete sections. It is an aggregate, rather than an organic whole, but a stridently articulated assemblage nonetheless—a curious combination of

---

17. McPherson (2014) 117–24 compares the process to the Greek conception of *hubris* in which excessive human ambition is followed by inevitable catastrophe at the hands of the gods.

18. *Works and Days*, 57–58, 252–53.

weak text and strong voice. One way to approach this combination is characterologically: Perses, the poet's brother, is the poem's addressee. He is either too stupid or too depraved to listen, hence the shoutiness, which wouldn't be necessary if he were not the way he is.

That said, Perses' obstinacy consists at least in part in his unwillingness to undertake the work that the gods have measured out for their inferiors (397–99). There is a suggestion that his refusal to do his allotted share is an ontological rebellion against the conditions of human life under Olympian rule. The same urgency informs the poet's advice when he is no longer explicitly addressing his brother but gathering information about how to put together a plow or how to transport goods in a wagon. Saving the technology of the present for posterity's benefit is a regular mytheme of postapocalyptic fiction, and from this perspective, Hesiod is looking ahead. He has the next apocalypse in mind.

The Byzantine scholar John Tzetzes observed that Hesiod anachronistically projects human sailing back into the mythological era of Prometheus. Commenting on Tzetzes' observation, Tim Rood, Carol Atack, and Tom Phillips reflect that, "by mixing temporal domains, Hesiod allows Perses and his listeners to imagine the events of the primordial past through the tools they use in their own lives."[19] Imagining human being as constituted by tool use is both a survival strategy and a way of conceptualizing a continuum of humanness through the multiple destructions of the successive forms of humankind. Anachronism allows the reader to seize upon the salient fact of technology by foregrounding a discordant instance. The idea that there have been and always will be humans like ourselves gives human beings something to survive for.

Modern postapocalyptic fiction frequently imagines technology loss in the form of what Edward Shanks, in *The People of the*

---

19. Rood, Atack, and Phillips (2020).

Ruins, called a "glissade."[20] The apocalyptic event, whatever it is, causes human beings to collapse back through multiple stages of technological achievement. When the knowledge that makes operational the technology of the present is lost, the survivors do not return to the previous generation's level, because no one in the present generation knows how to make or use the tools of the previous generation. People who drive tractors do not know how to make plows out of wood. Instead, human beings slip back rapidly to some kind of subsistence level at which people can figure out basic survival again, more or less from scratch.

Shelley has her own version of this story, but Hesiod's is more tightly focused on tool use and work as co-constitutive of humanness. His advice to his brother is "don't think, work" (299–319). It is not just that work makes you rich, and wealth is the basis of all forms of social esteem. Work has immediate consequences for mentality. An unsound or impaired mind is cured simply by working (315). Occupation is prior to mentation. Saving the knowledge of how to build a plow, or how to move goods in a wagon, is therefore not only a material backstop to the technological glissade. Preserving the ways of working that these things allow means the version of being human that Hesiod cares about can also be preserved in an unknowable future. Rousseau's wish to locate a moment of ideal balance between communal resources and individual capability is more urgently framed from a postapocalyptic perspective. It is not a matter of knowing when you would prefer to stop but when you have to stop, before humanness is lost altogether.

Hesiod's technological conservatism takes shape against the background of divine hostility that also informs his community politics. Since the gods are always looking for opportunities to afflict human beings, even a single bad actor can bring pestilence and famine upon his people. And since organized human life can be reduced to ruins in a moment by the gods' whimsical

---

20. Shanks (2012) 69.

malevolence, every single human being had better know how to build a plow or load a wagon, because they may very well have to. The community politics of modern postapocalyptic fiction covers the full gamut from solitary survivalism to ontological communitarianism, depending on how the individual author determines human beings' likelihood to work together in the face of disaster. Hesiod is at the pessimistic end of this spectrum. If you don't know what kind of wood to use for an axle, and what kind to use for a felloe, the goods you have husbanded, harvested, and stored will spill out onto the roadside when your wagon hits a rut, and you yourself will starve, providing an occasion for derision to your more capable neighbors.[21] This is a regular mytheme of postapocalyptic fiction. Avatars of Hesiod's precarious wagon continue to populate its worlds, from the handcart of J. D. Beresford's *Goslings* to the dysfunctional shopping carts of Paul Auster's *In the Country of Last Things*, Cormac McCarthy's *The Road*, and Octavia Butler's *Parable of the Sower*.[22]

To repeat, then, *Works and Days* is a weak text with a strong voice. In contrast to the realist novel, which is meant to instantiate and exemplify predictive probability through the entailments of character and plot, Hesiod's poem is a compendium of themes and motifs held together by the force of the poet's voice. But like the convergence of strong form and weak voice in the realist novel, which favors showing over telling and is optimistic about our ability to draw real-world conclusions from its limited sphere of operations, the convergence of weak text and strong voice in *Works and Days* also stages the truth of its represented world. Human cognition is feeble almost to the point of uselessness in its capacity to apprehend and represent the operations of the life-threatening cosmic whole.

This is the mode of understanding Ghosh calls catastrophism. Hesiod himself admits that his best claim to authority is that he

---

21. *Works and Days* 423–26, 692–93.
22. Curtis (2010) 17–20 gives examples.

has observed more in the way of local conditions than most people are able to because of the unusual travels he has undertaken as a wandering bard—another staple of postapocalyptic fiction from David Brin's *The Postman* to Emily St. John Mandel's *Station Eleven*. But for that very reason the poet is even more uncertain than others about the nature of the whole. More extensive observation does not lead to greater certainty or more secure judgment. Just the opposite, in fact. The text we know as *Works and Days* is the gestalt of an anxious mind haunted by the possibility of disaster on a cosmic scale but unable to offer more than bits and pieces by way of explanation and advice. It can only speculate about the evils that wander the earth under Zeus's recognizance; the vision of the whole is the property of the divine assailant alone.

When it first appeared in 1826, *The Last Man* was derided for being stupidly cruel.[23] Surfeit with apocalyptic visions was partly responsible for the censure. However, prompting readers to judge whether humanity's punishment fits its crimes is part of the role poets take on when they offer themselves as "unacknowledged legislators of the world." In "On Naïve and Sentimental Poetry," Friedrich Schiller claimed that poets represent Nature in periods when humanity loses touch with its own naturalness: "By virtue of the very notion of a poet, poets are everywhere the guardians of nature. Where they can no longer completely be this, and where they have already experienced within themselves the destructive influence of arbitrary and artificial forms or have had to contend with them, they will appear as nature's witnesses and avengers. They will either be nature or seek the lost nature."[24]

Schiller's idea would prove attractive to poets in the century to come. In "A Defence of Poetry," Percy Shelley argued that poets' action on behalf of Nature has a proto-institutional character as legal representation. Because poets are "mirrors of the gigantic

23. Synder (1978) 435; Paley (1993) 108.
24. Schiller (1998) 196.

shadows which futurity casts upon the present," poetry retains its archaic function as prophetic legislation even in modernity. Insofar as they are poets and allow the faculty of imagination to operate as a capability distinct from their quotidian moral commitments, poets are ahead of their time and outside history as such. What poetry wills as "the great instrument of moral good" and "institutor of human life" is representative, in both a literary and a legal sense, of a form of life to come, with moral sentiments that are more capacious than the society in which poets find themselves. As such, it is more truly reflective of the real thinking that takes place in the moral imagination of humanity at large than the parochial laws of their own time and place: "Poets are the unacknowledged legislators of the world."[25]

In developing this argument, Shelley reiterates the conflation of juridical roles in Schiller's conception of poets as "nature's witnesses and avengers." As part of his revisioning of the poet's quasi-legal authority within a society that has lost touch with human naturalness, he includes a second-order reflection on how a third party might judge a poet's right to speak for what is rightless in the future tense: "Let us for a moment stoop to the arbitration of popular breath, and usurping and uniting in our own persons the incompatible characters of accuser, witness, judge, and executioner, let us decide without trial, testimony, or form, that certain motives of those who are 'there sitting where we dare not soar,' are reprehensible."[26]

Shelley takes upon himself the task of negotiating between first-personal conviction and third-personal judgment. A potential obstacle to the imagination becomes a moment of access in staging the total drama of the poetic representation of Nature. Once the question of Nature casts the poet within the legal imaginary, the full spectrum of juridical roles becomes available for

---

25. Shelley (2003) 677, 682, 699–701. Compare Hölderlin's claim in "Andenken": "Was bleibet aber, stiften die Dichter."

26. Shelley (2003) 699.

performance. The first-personal character of poetic representation of Nature is not limited to the roles of witness and avenger. The poet wishes to enact in imagination the future justice of which he is the distant mirror, but his awareness that, as one of the "unacknowledged legislators of the world," he has no actual juridical power displaces this enactment to a fictional show trial of his fitness for the work he would accomplish on Nature's behalf.

Mary Shelley evinces no such doubts. *The Last Man* finds humanity wanting and takes justice into its own hands. However, unlike, say, M. P. Shiel's *The Purple Cloud*, which exults in the orgiastic destruction of humanity, Shelley's novel lingers ruefully with its remnant population in the moments of its passing, dwelling with what might have been, rather than gloating over the end of what was.

Could it be that this tarrying with the remnant is actually the novel's greatest cruelty? For a work that draws so deeply on Hesiod for its understanding of human limitation to present the return of Greek mythology, not simply as the best that human beings can hope for, but as a kind of idyll in Nature, surely begs the question. The answer will depend on how we understand the cognitive status of the return of the gods in *The Last Man*, and this question is difficult to answer definitively. On one hand, the return of the gods is a direct outcome of the survivors' postapocalyptic occupations. On the other, it is increasingly obvious to all of them that their days are numbered. The natural entities they deify at the end of days don't actually care for them in return. Their proximity to Greek mythology has the feeling of fiction, but is it a fiction willingly entertained, perhaps for the purposes of consolation, or is it a pernicious delusion, another gift of Pandora? Is their new relationality with the things of Nature a form of false consciousness, a way of shielding themselves from the hostile reality of Nature?

The answer to the question does not matter all that much to the survivors themselves. It is only in the light of later postapocalyptic fiction that its undecidability gains salience, even urgency. Postapocalyptic fiction wants no gap between occupation and mentation; survivalist fiction makes active participation in ontological reflection a basic fitness test for survival. *The Last Man*, because it is a last man novel, remains agnostic. There is no time in which to work out what the right answer would have been. The peculiar pathos of *The Last Man* is due to the fact that Shelley's Nature, unlike Hesiod's Zeus, is a process, not a person. It has no animosity to human beings and eradicates them without relief or remorse—without feelings of any kind, in fact—so that these affects now belong to the poet who acts as Nature's proxy.

Why the gods keep on creating human beings if they are only going to decreate them is likewise a question that Hesiod does not try to answer. *Phthonos* is simply a fact of life for human beings under Olympian rule. The gods have destroyed humankind numerous times in the past, and they will destroy them again in the future. The successive remakings do, however, raise another question—what is the human thing that persists through these remakings?—and this question Hesiod does answer. It is by virtue of a persistent negative exceptionalism that human beings regard themselves as an entity that persists.[27] However the more divinely favored versions of humankind may have lived on the earth, human beings are now the least well equipped for survival of all living beings. Technological dependency is the ontological horizon of humanness. No plows and wagons means no human beings, only featherless bipeds (to use Plato's expression) squabbling over scraps in the road.

Shelley draws on Hesiod's negative exceptionalism for her vision of postapocalyptic life, but unlike Hesiod, she imagines the apocalyptic event as final: the Last Man is the last man, and Nature, having decreated, will not create again. The idea that there might be successive humankinds, who somehow remain essentially human throughout their multiple remakings, is taken up again in the twentieth century by Olaf Stapledon in *Last and First Men*, in which he offers a massive, secularized extension of Hesiod's vision: eighteen kinds of human beings who last some two

---

27. On negative exceptionalism in Lucretius and the Epicurean tradition, see Holmes (2013).

billion years into the future until they are at last eradicated. Throughout this history, "the species remained essentially human."[28] Stapledon pushes down the task of figuring out in virtue of what this claim of essential continuity holds true from the author to the human beings who are his characters and readers. The persistent rediscovery of humanness is the plot that is enacted in the novel's cosmic timescale, its protagonist the species being of humankind as a whole.

Stapledon's Fourth Men, for example, remake their humanity by transforming themselves into gigantic brains without limbs. They live inside ferro-concrete brain turrets, where their survival needs are mechanically supplied, until they eventually realize that this life of pure cerebration is a mistake. They do not merely suffer from "intellectual limitation" as a result of their circumscribed existence; their lack of a body is the cause of "the limitation of their insight into values." Having attained the understanding that mentation depends on occupation, they create a reembodied successor race to supplant themselves, but these Fifth Men increasingly devote their activities to a project of inhabiting the reality of the past as lived experience and are finally haunted to death by the horrors in which they have chosen to participate.[29]

For the Fifth Men, ontological speculation proves counteradaptive for survival. Indeed, the drive toward extremity inherent in a dialectical reaction to the past ensures that the history of humankind is a story of close encounters with extinction. Rather than being adaptable in a way that tends toward easy survival—choosing what it will become so as to make the best of local affordances—humankind extrapolates differential tendencies from out of itself. Its life history is one of essential seriality because of the tendency in each successive form of itself to develop an extreme version of its own possibilities.

---

28. Stapledon (2008) 142.
29. Stapledon (2008) 166, 182–83. The Sixteenth Men take a more activist approach, "a crusade to liberate the past" (212).

In *Last and First Men*, succession is a processual outcome of human decision-making. There is no Zeus or Nature figure in which the transformations of humankind originate. Stapledon uses symphonic music to figure the species being that persists through these changes and whose fullness of being is only apprehensible when we contemplate the mutations of its local forms. We readers are "tremors in the opening bars" of this music, and the humankinds to come are its movements. The visionary prophet of the final, Eighteenth Men takes up the musical figure again in his retrospective framing of the narrative we have just read, fusing it with the apocalyptic image of flowering and a Hesiodic emphasis on the limits of human cognition:

> Man was winged hopefully. He had in him to go further than this short flight, now ending. He proposed even that he should become the Flower of All Things, and that he should learn to be the All-Knowing, the All-Admiring. Instead, he is to be destroyed. He is only a fledgling caught in a bush-fire. He is very small, very simple, very little capable of insight. His knowledge of the great orb of things is but a fledgling's knowledge. His admiration is a nestling's admiration for the things kindly to his own small nature. He delights only in food and the food-announcing call. The music of the spheres passes over him, through him, and is not heard. Yet it has used him. And now it uses his destruction. Great, and terrible, and very beautiful is the Whole; and for man the best is that the Whole should use him.[30]

The prophet checks his metaphor—"Does it really use him? Is the beauty of the Whole really enhanced by our agony?"—only to reassert its validity with greater conviction:

> Throughout all his existence man has been striving to hear the music of the spheres, and has seemed to himself once and again

---

30. Stapledon (2008) 246.

to catch some phrase of it, or even a hint of the whole form of it. Yet he can never be sure that he has truly heard it, nor even that there is any such perfect music at all to be heard. Inevitably so, for if it exists, it is not for him in his littleness. But one thing is certain. Man himself, at the very least, is music, a brave theme that makes music also of its vast accompaniment, its matrix of storms and stars. Man himself in his degree is eternally a beauty in the eternal form of things. It is very good to have been man. And so we may go forward together with laughter in our hearts, and peace, thankful for the past, and for our own courage. For we shall make after all a fair conclusion to this brief music that is man.

Stapledon oscillates here, as he does elsewhere in *Last and First Men*, between the idea that being fully human is becoming the consciousness of the cosmos—its principle of self-reflection and self-understanding—and the idea that being fully human is becoming the mind of the human superorganism—a synopsis of all human views, but not cosmic consciousness itself. In other works, Stapledon uses the figure of the plant to articulate what is at stake for human self-experience in each of these alternatives, and it is worth looking briefly at the role of this figure in his lesser-known short stories before turning to the novel *Star Maker*, in which the "vegetable humanities" figure an alternative mode of accommodation to humankind's successive remakings, in contrast to the interpersonal encounter with the cosmic being in whom these remakings originate.

The protagonist of Stapledon's story "The Man Who Became a Tree" falls asleep one day beneath a beech tree, and his understanding of natural processes converges with that of the tree:

> He now felt that his deep participation in this great tree's life had opened up to him a sphere vaster than his unaided human consciousness could ever penetrate, and far vaster than the life merely of all vegetation. It was as though the plants, with their less individualized consciousness, were constantly open to the

divine; as though, one and all, they were not really individuals at all, but rather (so he figuratively expressed it to himself) limbs and sense organs of God. But that strange "openness to the divine," in which all vegetation easily shared was far too difficult for his analytic human intelligence to grasp."[31]

Staging the expansion of human understanding to cosmic scale as becoming vegetal is an idea with ancient roots. In Heraclitus's "nature loves to hide" (DK B123) and "an unapparent connection is stronger than an apparent one" (DK B54), the inconspicuous ubiquity of vegetal life figures the nature of the cosmos as a lifeworld that is equally alive in all its parts. So too for Plotinus, at the other end of the Greek philosophical tradition, plants are less obviously arranged as a set of organs in a hierarchical processing arrangement than animals are. Their living activity appears to us to operate with equal force throughout their bodies, so that their presence alongside us affords us a regular opportunity to reflect on the dispersed activity of life in the cosmos as a whole, as opposed to its intense concentration in the eyes of an animal or the face of a human being.[32]

Like the life of a plant, the life of the cosmos is everywhere at once as a signal of its being a home for other life-forms, so that Plotinus can identify the way human beings make themselves at home in it with the way worms make themselves at home in a rotting cabbage (*Ennead* 4.3.4). The homeliness of the cosmos does not manifest itself in the mode of an artifact, like a house that has been designed for human use, but rather in the mode of life. Its self-disclosure is the signaling of one living organism to another that it is available to it to inhabit. The cosmos as plant stands for

---

31. Stapledon (1997) 131.

32. Marder (2013) 27–50 traces the history of this thought from Heraclitus's *physis* that "loves to hide" to vegetal life as "dispersed spirit" in Hegel and Nietzsche. Understood positively, rather than as a form of privation with respect to the being of animals, "the dispersed life of plants is a mode of being in relation to all the others, being *qua* being-with" (50).

the ability to recognize the livingness of the lifeworld as a home that comes into being from the source of life as itself alive, or to misrecognize it as a creation, a disposition of matter that is put together for its inhabitants in a more or less satisfactory way as craftwork.

Human beings cannot fully apprehend the livingness of the lifeworld as their home when they are at home in it, precisely because it is a relationship between the living and the living. It is not seen properly if they think to view it from the outside, as in the contemplation of a nonliving material object.[33] Plotinus likens our apprehension of belonging to it to a dancer's momentary understanding of their participation in a chorus when they are briefly turned toward the center of its movement (*Ennead* 6.9.8). The evanescence of our apprehension of belonging to the world should not be understood as a problem for our self-experience but as integral to the form of relationality that is proper to the life-form that we are. Captivated by our own animality, we are only momentarily able to look aside from it, to stand outside it and experience ourselves as subjects of vegetality, like living beings as a whole.

In "The Man Who Became a Tree," the *ecstasis* that becoming vegetal affords is grounded in an initial immunological isolation from other human beings. The protagonist is an "inveterate escapist" who "carefully avoided forming lasting ties with man or woman."[34] His cosmic consciousness is achieved through the transcendence of local care, but the cosmos is by nature amenable to the rescaling of human understanding that this transcendence affords. In *Last and First Men*, the fusion of music and flowering that figures the expansion of human cognition to cosmic scale is a parting gesture, the backward glance of humankind's last prophet as he surveys the fully unfolded efflorescence of the "fair spirit,

---

33. Compare the convolutions that the creature in Kafka's "The Burrow" puts itself through as it tries to apprehend its home from the outside as something it has made for itself deliberately, rather than as a phenotypical enactment of itself.

34. Stapledon (1997) 129.

whom a star conceived and a star kills." More grimly, in Stapledon's short story "A World of Sound," music is not merely a figure of achieved consciousness that signals the end of days for humankind. Participation in the music of the spheres is the very thing that alerts the cosmos to human presence, and when awakened, this hostile lifeworld seeks out the hiding place of the parasite lodged in its own body by a kind of echolocation in order to destroy it:

> The brute was now moving more slowly, nosing in search of me as it approached. Presently it lay immediately below me, far down in the bass. Its body was now all too clearly heard as a grim cacophony of growling and belching. Its strident tentacles moved beneath me like the waving tops of trees beneath a man clinging to a cliff face. Still searching, it passed on beneath me. Such was my relief that I lost consciousness for a moment and slipped several octaves down before I could recover myself. The movement revealed my position. The beast of prey returned, and began clambering awkwardly toward me. Altitude soon checked its progress, but it reached me with one tentacle, one shrieking arpeggio. Desperately I tried to withdraw myself farther into the treble, but the monster's limb knit itself into the sound-pattern of my flesh. Frantically struggling, I was dragged down, down into the suffocating bass. There, fangs and talons of sound tore me agonizingly limb from limb.

The sleeper of "A World of Sound" awakens from the lifeworld of music just in the nick of time, but in his dream horror, music figures an allergic reaction to the rescaling of human consciousness on the part of the cosmos itself. Plotinus argues that for plants, stars, microbes, and the earth itself, their form of life is their mode of contemplation (*Enneads* 3.8.1). It is a mode from which human beings are excluded by their form of life as rational animals who have to activate contemplation as a special mode of cognition different from the kinds of mentation they typically employ in their projective, goal-oriented, conative activities. Stapledon offers a truly Gnostic version of this negative exceptionalism here, as the activation of such cognition does not simply block human consciousness from participation in the lifeworld as a whole, but exposes a weaker life-form to predation by a stronger. Thinking with the cosmos is not merely maladaptive but suicidal.

Stapledon makes extensive use of cognitive signaling as a narrative device in *Star Maker*. The novel's structure and characterology has much in common with "The Man Who Became a Tree." Its protagonist falls asleep on a hillside near his home and then finds himself on a quest for humanlike life-forms in the cosmos as a whole. Here, too, the expansion of understanding that is figured as becoming vegetal has an immunological grounding. In order to become "the growing point of the cosmical spirit," an "organ of exploration, a feeler," he must break his attachment to his "trivial earthly life," including his wife and children, even while such forms of attachment are the metric by which the humanness of life elsewhere is judged as a "silver" or "golden" age in comparison to human achievements on earth.[35]

The protagonist of *Star Maker* eventually joins forces with the roving consciousnesses of other humanlike life-forms, and they understand themselves to be "playing a small part in one of the great movements by which the cosmos was seeking to know itself, and even see beyond itself," as they use their shared cognition to home in on, and navigate toward, welcoming signals from other humanlike minds. The journey reframes what seemed to be an enormous expansion of realist narrative ambition in *Last and First Men* as a brief moment in the voyagers' apprehension of cosmic duration. The entire scope of the earlier novel occupies a single paragraph in *Star Maker*. We see humankind "blunder through many alternating phases of dullness and lucidity" on earth, changing its bodily shape from epoch to epoch "as a cloud changes," struggle with Martian invaders, relocate to Venus and Neptune, then be "burnt up like a moth in a flame by irresistible catastrophe."

35. Stapledon (2008) 17–18, 41–46, 53–54.

All this striving and transformation is accomplished in the space of four sentences.[36]

Imagining the full array of humanlike life-forms above and beyond the perdurance of human species being that is the imaginative project of *Last and First Men* affords Stapledon a larger set of possibilities for staging modes of cognitive and affective accommodation to the life of the cosmos as a whole. The plant-men his travelers encounter seem to have achieved a particularly happy balance between animal and vegetable modes of being. During the day, they spread their leaves to the sun. Not only do they directly absorb "the essential elixir of life which animals receive only at second hand in the mangled flesh of their prey," they also participate in the form of cosmic contemplation proper to plants: they maintain "immediate physical contact with the source of cosmical being," and this contact, though physical, is "also in some sense spiritual." In this state of quasisexual union with the cosmos, each of the plant-men alike experiences "an ecstasy in which subject and object seemed to become identical, an ecstasy of subjective union with the obscure source of all finite being," which is also a mode of *theoria*, a contemplative appreciation of their own species being in relation to living beings as a whole: "He mentally reviewed every kind of human conduct with detached contemplative joy, as a factor in the universe."[37]

In the course of time, the plant-men lose the balance between the plant and animal components of their nature. Having swerved toward animal life, they then veer too far toward vegetal life and are "undone by the extravagance of their own mystical quietism." The "vegetable humanities" they instantiate turn out to be a rarity among cosmic life-forms as a whole, and the explorers themselves are increasingly drawn into the quest for a face-to-face, interpersonal form of relationality with the Star Maker in whom the cosmos originates, as the form of relationality proper to their own

---

36. Stapledon (2008) 54, 133.
37. Stapledon (2008) 92–93.

kind of mentation. The Star Maker they eventually encounter in the novel's "supreme moment" is a maker who tires of his own creations, much like Hesiod's Zeus. He does not destroy what he has made but puts it aside in the boundless space of the universe as he turns to his next creation.[38]

The exploring minds struggle to articulate their response to the divinity that externalizes and realizes itself in successive creation. His is the fullness of being that in *First and Last Men* was the species being of humankind apprehended in its transformative efflorescence through eighteen successive local forms. Contemplation is the Star Maker's natural occupation, but the project of apprehending it ends in ineffability. The protagonist is drawn to adore him, but the movement falls short, and the sleeper awakens on the hillside where the story began. Although rightly understood as both a personal being and a process, the Star Maker offers no lasting affordances for musical participation in his life.

---

38. Stapledon (2008) 128, 95, 168.

2

The Persistence of Memory

IN ANTIQUITY, Hesiod's postapocalyptic humanism prepared the ground for speculative anthropology. In book 3 of *Laws,* Plato suggests that "the world of men has often been destroyed by floods, plagues, and many other things, in such a way that only a small portion of the human race has survived." He ponders how isolated mountain dwellers might have been able to reconstitute historical forms of sociality after a flood wiped out humankind in the cultivated plains below.[1] As is said explicitly in the case of theology,[2] poetic thinking opens a field that political science settles and populates. Speculative anthropology forwards a conversation about the form of life that best serves human capabilities which began before philosophy as such entered upon the scene.

It is, however, Aristotle's student Dicaearchus who makes the largest claims for poetry's vision of the deep past as an image of human happiness to come. Aristotle had claimed that the polis, with its hierarchical division of labor, was the form of life in which human beings could best realize the capabilities that are naturally theirs. The city, in fact, is ontologically prior to singular human beings, because it is only in cities that there is really such a thing as a human being whose natural limits and capabilities can be investigated. Dicaearchus, by contrast, argued that human beings

---

1. *Laws* 3.677a–682e.
2. *Laws* 10.886b.

were more fully themselves before the invention of the polis, and they should look to poetry to understand the reasons why.

Dicaearchus was an innovator within a well-established ancient tradition of speculative anthropology. He migrated to mainland Greece from his birthplace in Sicily, and the title of his best-known work, *The Life of Greece*, is unprecedented in a work of Deep History, suggesting a desire to write the story of his adoptive homeland as if it were the biography of a person with a distinctive form of life. Like other Peripatetic thinkers, he uses poetic quotations as evidence, but the way he uses Hesiod is remarkable within this philosophical tradition of thinking with poetry. As the most recent modern editor of his work observes, "a remarkable strategy" can be seen in his account of the poet's myth of the Golden Age in *Works and Days*, for he holds the myth to contain "a kernel of truth if adequately rationalized."[3] But it is not merely the extent to which Dicaearchus is willing to credit the details in Hesiod that is remarkable. In apocalyptic thought, a kernel is the remaindered core of the past, gathered and garnered, from which an alternative future may be regrown. To describe Dicaearchus as finding a kernel of truth in Hesiod is to place him in a tradition of regenerative vegetal thinking, which meshes intuitively with his distinctive understanding of Hesiod and the deep past.

Rather than seeing the earliest humans as hunter-gatherers, who were superseded by pastoralists and agriculturalists, Dicaearchus proposes his own version of the three-stage model of universal history he inherited from earlier Greek thinkers. The first humans were gatherers, pure and simple, and hunting and pastoralism emerged together at a later date as ways of "laying hands on animals." In this way, he is able to harmonize his story of human development with Hesiod's claim that in the Golden Age everything grew of its own accord, and human beings were peaceable to one another and to other animals. There was no hunting, and no accumulation of food supplies that could have led to conflict

---

3. Verhasselt (2018) 7–8, 50.

between human beings. It was by "laying hands on animals" for the sake of domestication that human beings gave themselves the idea of enslaving one another, so that "simultaneously with the wrong-doing against animals, war and the desire to possess more than others slipped in."[4]

The excess of material goods produced by the ensuing large-scale civilizations had deleterious consequences. At the macrosocial level, intrastate inequality and interstate covetousness led to insurrections and wars. Internally, in the psychic life of the individual, the craving for distinction (φιλοτιμία) generated by social inequality estranged human beings from their natural goods by outsourcing pleasure in their own capabilities to the judgment of others—Rousseau's fatal substitution of the *amour de soi* common to human beings and animals with the *amour-propre* that can only be provided by social recognition.

Human beings live a debilitated life in comparison to what they are capable of, whereas once upon a time they lived in a Golden Age, without the intra- and interspecies oppression that characterize civilization in the present. The people of Deep History left no records, so apprehending why their life was more satisfying to them requires attunement to forms of life that can only be reinhabited imaginatively. As part of this speculative project, poetic fictions must be sifted for evidence about living conditions prior to the invention of the polis, including the idea that before domestication, human beings and animals enjoyed a common freedom. If poetry's obviously fantastic accretions are removed, what remains are memories of lived experience presented beneath a protective veil of fiction, and which may perhaps be recovered for the future. Dicaearchus fuses the horizons of philosophical and literary anthropology to uncover the desire for a more satisfying form of life that is the common drive of both in their access to the past: "Life under Cronus was of this kind—since it is necessary to accept that it did exist, that is has not been renowned to no purpose,

---

4. Verhasselt (2018) 231–35; Lovejoy and Boas (1935) 94–96.

but also, by laying aside what is excessively mythical, to reduce it to natural terms based on reason."[5]

At the end of the rainbow of speculative anthropology lies ancient philosophy's pot of gold: not the relational self-regard of the citizen that originates in diverse achievements, but the full-body contentment of the sage that comes from being able to do for oneself all the things a human being need do in order to live a happy life. Given the fragmentary condition of Dicaearchus's work, which survives only in quotations by other authors, it is sometimes difficult to know to what extent the citing author's thinking overlaps with his own, and to what extent the citer is imposing his own ways of thinking on the cited. Crucially, though, it is clear that what Dicaearchus valued in Hesiod's account of the Golden Age is the autarkic quality of early life. Since early humans only ate what offered itself of its own accord, they were free of the cares of agriculture and hunting. Even the poverty of their food supply was a secondary benefit, as it spared them the ill-health and metabolic disruptions endemic to contemporary civilization's diet of cultivated grains and cooked food, especially meat.[6]

---

5. Dicaearchus 56A, in Fortenbaugh and Schütrumpf (2001) 63–65.

6. The major fragment of *The Life of Greece* in which Dicaearchus sets out his view of the life of early humans is a citation in the vegetarian Platonist Porphyry's *On Abstinence*. Saunders (2001) 247–48 argues that the paucity of the food supply at this time according to Dicaearchus means that he cannot himself be praising this life, and that his own views need to be distinguished both from those of Porphyry and from those of Hesiod whom he is citing. Hesiod, Saunders argues, is the reason that contemporaries of Dicaearchus continued to believe that the life of early humans was superior to their own, a view Dicaearchus wishes to demonstrate is false. As Verhasselt (2018) 241 points out, however, "the absence of abundant food is part of this life of bliss, since it resulted in a healthy diet," and Dicaearchus himself "explicitly calls the primitive life happy" in this fragment. To which I would add that, while Saunders certainly appreciates that the main thrust of Dicaearchus's account is "to present the life of early man as autarkic," it is difficult to see how it can be construed as "only minimally autarkic," given how much more free from dependence on others his early humans are in comparison to human beings of the present.

In *A Declaration of the Rights of Human Beings*, Raoul Vaneigem begins his rethinking of the rights tradition by reiterating the importance of Golden Age thinking for a just assessment of human well-being:

> The legends of the Golden Age, as well as a good number of utopias, have been fueled by the obscure memory of pre-agrarian civilization, where the economy of the gatherer allowed women such a prominent role that it fostered a society in symbiosis with nature, and in which violence had no place other than through occasional recourse to the hunt. The very idea of the Golden Age runs counter to the prevalence of conquering, well-muscled virility in the Bronze and Iron Ages, which embarked upon the rape of women and the earth, and engendered the toiling, warrior race whose stunted remains have set down, as the final chapter in their history, the infamy of concentration camps and the annihilation of natural resources.[7]

Vaneigem is entirely in keeping with Hesiod and Dicaearchus in viewing the present as the long extenuation of the Age of Iron and in believing that poetry preserves an "obscure memory" of better times. Where he differs from these ancient thinkers, however, is in the absence of the idea of autarky from his account of what made the Golden Age better than our own. Vaneigem is an ontological futurist. A constant refrain of *A Declaration of the Rights of Human Beings* is the injunction to "leave behind the context of survival." The human beings whose rights he is declaring have creation as "the way of being of human life." They exist not merely to embody the life force inherent in all earthly beings but to transcend, transform, and re-create it.[8] Survival is the mere

---

7. Vaneigem (2019) 3.

8. Vaneigem (2019) 14, 41, 65–67. Cf. Vaneigem (1998) 11, 16–17, where the free spirit, like the true self of Thoreau's *Walden*, emerges through close observation of the difference between mere survival and really living.

stub of being human, whereas for Hesiod, Dicaearchus, and the greatest continuer of their thinking, Rousseau, being able to fulfill one's survival needs for oneself is the ineliminable basis of happiness. This is what the autarky of the individual human being means, and it is this version of being human that is embraced as a prosocial capability in postapocalyptic fiction, and not just in its explicitly survivalist modes. Autarky is the foundation of forms of collective life that provide lasting happiness for human beings, not their opposite.

What Dicaearchus sees in Hesiod's account of the Golden Age is a pre-theoretical memory of the virtuous circle of early life. Simple provisioning means simple forms of self-care in which everyone can be competent. Knowing you can take care of yourself means being able to take pleasure in the simple fact of your own existence, without the anxiety of outsourcing your subsistence to others. Rousseau compares the happiness of indigenous Americans to the *ataraxia* (freedom from care) of the ancient Stoics. The inhabitant of the New World is still "carrying all of himself along with him."[9] This belief in a fundamental human capability that might be recovered for the life of tomorrow structures the project of speculative anthropology from antiquity all the way to Rousseau, Claude Lévi-Strauss, and Pierre Clastres.

In *Society against the State*, Clastres keenly appreciates the safeguarding of autarky as a fundamental principle of the indigenous societies of South America. The deliberate limitation of a society's productive forces to providing its members with what they need to subsist ensures surplus time for creative mentation and other nonproductive activities. It also prevents the accumulation of surplus goods that might lead to conflict and forestalls the emergence of a state based on division of labor in which each member is no longer capable of fulfilling their survival needs for themselves. Clastres reiterates the virtuous circle of ancient speculative

---

9. Rousseau (1997) 135.

anthropology. Golden Age economy subtends a particular form of life:

> There is nothing in the economic working of a primitive society, a society without a State, that enables a difference to be introduced making some richer or poorer than others, because no one in such a society feels the quaint desire to do more, own more, or appear to be more than his neighbor. The ability, held by all cultures alike, to satisfy their material needs, and the exchange of goods and services, which continually prevents the private accumulation of goods, quite simply make it impossible for such a desire—the desire for possession that is actually the desire for power—to develop. Primitive society, the first society of abundance, leaves no room for the desire for overabundance.[10]

Clastres will ask himself Rousseau's question—how could such a society be dissolved from within so that the state ceased to be impossible?—but he does not attempt an answer to the state's mysterious origin, focusing instead on the still apprehensible conditions of its nonemergence—the figure of the chief who is the opposite of the figure of the despot, insofar as he instantiates forms of persuasion without the force of law or coercion—and the continuing appeal of the small, face-to-face, self-contained societies these conditions enable.[11]

Clastres emphasizes the political structures of indigenous South America. His claim that these avert the emergence of the hierarchical state—whose foundation is the accumulation and unequal distribution of goods through division of labor—complements the focus on capabilities and their loss in Rousseau's and Lévi-Strauss's theorizations of the speculative Neolithic. We cathect to it because we apprehend intuitively that it had attained a certain threshold of security with regard to cold, hunger, and

10. Clastres (1989) 204–205.
11. Clastres (1989) 205–13.

rest, but without the hypertrophic development of social life in which a person is shorn of their best capabilities as a human animal.[12] The reason the social bonds of Golden Age society are so strong is because each of its members is capable of surviving independently, not because they need each other in order to survive. As in the new forms of social life that postapocalyptic fiction imagines, the forms of social life here are willingly embraced. Belonging and caring are choices, not obligations of mutual dependence. If this is the age at which we wish our species had stopped, Clastres shows us how it actually stopped itself, through specific social institutions that prevent the emergence of the state.

The depressive anthropology of Rousseau, Lévi-Strauss, and Clastres is a speculative project, but one that is provoked by concrete examples. Without the encounter with the New World and its inhabitants, Europeans would never have thought to interrogate their own form of life as a loss of capabilities, and it is this reflection on loss that should be the starting point for the criticism of social organization in the present. It is only by apprehending what we lack that we can know what to aim for, and it is only by looking inside after first looking outside that we can appreciate what we lack. In the encounter with concrete possibilities, the debilitated self of the polis can recognize what is denied to it in its present state of incapacity and acknowledge its desire for a fuller existence than it is presently capable of:

> Western Europe may have produced anthropologists precisely because it was a prey to strong feelings of remorse, which forced it to compare its image with those of different societies in the hope that they would show the same defects or would help to explain how its own defects had developed within it.... The anthropologist is the less able to ignore his own civilization and to dissociate himself from its faults in that his very existence is

---

12. Lévi-Strauss (1992) 391.

incomprehensible except as an attempt at redemption: he is the symbol of atonement.[13]

Lévi-Strauss's language of defect looks back to Rousseau's point of departure in *The Discourse on Inequality*, which begins with an epigraph from Aristotle's *Politics*: "What is natural has to be investigated not in beings that are depraved, but in those that are good according to nature." For Aristotle, this investigation does not entail trying to grasp what can hardly be known about distant times and faraway peoples. There would be no sense in a project such as Rousseau's, which seeks to discover what the civilization of the polis deprives people of through speculative reflection on forms of life outside or prior to it. Human beings at simpler levels of social organization are either wild animals or gods and do not belong to the study of the *anthropos* at all.

For Aristotle, human beings lend themselves to understanding, because they are everywhere present in the form of life that allows them to be recognized as what they truly are. Social form and cognitive ambition dovetail perfectly, whereas for Rousseau, having a cognitive ambition may be the very thing that makes its realization impossible. The contrast with Aristotle that his epigraph points up seems designed to focus attention on the difficulty of the speculative project he has set himself: "It is by dint of studying man that we have made it impossible to know him." There can be no question of identifying human possibilities with "the men we have before our eyes," as Aristotle does.[14] Getting to the "speculative Neolithic," as Lévi-Strauss calls it,[15] demands a different kind of practice than scientific study.

---

13. Lévi-Strauss (1992) 389, 414. Sontag (1961) claims that Lévi-Strauss's practice of anthropology as a "total occupation" remediates the experience of loss to some extent insofar as it is one of the few intellectual vocations that does not demand the "sacrifice of one's manhood."

14. Rousseau (1997) 124, 138.

15. Lévi-Strauss (1992) 391.

So while Rousseau frets about the limitations of his anthropological materials and worries that his European informants see only themselves in the non-European people they encounter, he is not consequently after more details. The closer you get to the object that troubles complacent resignation to your own form of life, the more effectively the mechanisms of repression kick in that prevent you from seeing it for what it really is. More information is not the solution to this self-denying response. What is required is a form of writing that can circumvent or deactivate it. Rousseau is a poeticist. He wants a way of representing capabilities that can forestall the immunological reaction by which his readers immediately metabolize ethnic difference as their own cultural superiority, so that they are turned back to the body and to the relationship between occupation and mentation in other forms of life:

> How are we to imagine the sort of pleasure that a savage takes in spending his life alone in the depths of forests, or fishing, or blowing into a poor flute without ever managing to draw a single note from it and without troubling to learn to do so?[16]

Rousseau has "flute" here (*flûte*) rather than, say, "calumet." Like Hesiod's mythological sailing, this passage is an exercise in anachronistic *détournement* that turns the ethnographic inquisition back on the would-be observer. Whether Rousseau means the pipe of the pastoral musician or the flute of the modern orchestra, the anachronism—or better, perhaps, anatopism—points readers back to their own misplaced assumptions about the value of particular occupations: "If the thing is useless, so is the labour contained in it; the labour does not count as labour, and therefore creates no value."[17] Justification of the present with reference to another time and place is refused, and we are left to reflect upon

---

16. Rousseau (1997) 219.
17. Marx (1990) 131.

the melancholic self-regard that set us on the path of inquiry in the first place.

In *Manifest Manners*, Gerald Vizenor argues that when anthropology loses touch with the ruefulness of its speculative origins, ethnographic description replaces the original self-critical project with "inventions of tribal cultures"—totalizing cultural simulations that threaten to lock indigenous peoples out of their own ways of being. Indigenous culture is made into a mirror of the reservation system by ethnographers who have forgotten that their own enterprise began in melancholy comparative assessments of human capabilities. When the origin is forgotten or disavowed, the "truancies and cruelties of a melancholy civilization" now extend even to the refusal to recognize its own depression in the face of New World possibilities:

> Native American Indian imagination and the pleasures of language games are disheartened in the manifest manners of documentation and the imposition of cultural representation; tribal testimonies are unheard, and tricksters, the wild ironies of survivance, transformation, natural reason, and liberation in stories, are marooned as obscure moral simulations in translations.[18]

Vizenor's understanding that melancholy informs the ethnographic project only in an occluded, frustrated form leads him to emphasize the trickster as a performative figure who works to undo the totalizing constructions of culture by ethnographic subjects who have lost touch with the depressive origin of their own occupation. His concept of survivance focuses on what people do, rather than what they think, as a way of pushing back against the de-agentification of the individual in totalizing ethnographic accounts of Indian culture. Mentality is overplayed in ethnographic description and becomes a form of determinism. Culture as ineluctable formation by received thought occludes the hope that is

---

18. Vizenor (1994) 13, 76.

preserved in the memory of what people actually did. Ethnography makes cultures into lost causes, closed domains that survivors can never hope to enter, whereas trickster performance, insofar as it is a practice—doing something with the body—is a portal to historical memory recoverable from bodies in action.

The tension between anthropological melancholy and ethnographic substitution is recapitulated in postapocalyptic fiction in the degree of explicitness that is mobilized to produce the reader's imaginative assent to the world of the fiction. At one extreme, there is Ursula Le Guin's *Always Coming Home*, in which the languages, social structures, and characteristic forms of material culture of the societies of a northern California to come are depicted with a degree of detail that emulates academic ethnography. At the other, there are more or less deliberate instances of Rousseauian poeticism, which let readers access the relationship between occupation and mentation in another form of life without the excess of detail that might make its inhabitants seem altogether alien to them.

For ancient primitivists, fiction allows us to apprehend capabilities that are latent in ourselves by staging them as the life of the past. Under present circumstances we may not know what we are capable of, but cathexis to the anthropological record is itself a symptom of capability loss, Rousseau's "wish to be able to go backwards." *Latium*, the Hiding Place, is where Golden Age memories are tested for recovery. It is a place of concealment that was secreted away before "long roads made the land accessible to all." Saturn wished his home in Italy to be called Latium because there he had "safely lived in hiding [*latuisset*]." Its concealment in space is emblematic of its value for understanding Deep History. If human beings can access through poetry the life that is possible in such places, they can recover for themselves the life that their ancestors led there.[19]

---

19. Lovejoy and Boas (1935) 58–59. Cf. Le Guin (2019) 706 on the Golden Age conditions of indigenous California: "Being isolated from contact and protected from conquest are . . . characteristics of utopia."

In "On Naïve and Sentimental Poetry," Friedrich Schiller observes that the pastoral idyll is an example of the way in which speculative futures sometimes survive by going underground and presenting themselves as speculative pasts.[20] In "A Non-Euclidean View of California as a Cold Place to Be," Ursula Le Guin compares Schiller's understanding of the idyll as backward thinking about the future to the porcupine tales of Cree storytelling in which the porcupine "goes backward, looks forward." The porcupine "consciously goes backward in order to speculate safely on the future, allowing him to look out at his enemy or the new day." For the Cree, this is "an instructive act of self-preservation," and Le Guin associates her own writing with this regressive mode of speculative fiction: "In order to speculate safely on an inhabitable future, perhaps we would do well to find a rock crevice and go backward. In order to find our roots, perhaps we should look for them where roots are usually found."[21]

To operationalize the speculative anthropology of postapocalyptic fiction for the recovery of human capabilities, there must be trust that literary staging can in fact give access to the relationship between occupation and mentation in the forms of life it imagines—a willingness to entertain the belief that the optimal form of our human future is discoverable in the past as lived experience and that it can be reinhabited as such. The nature of the apocalyptic event determines whether the glissade through prior forms of historical life comes to a halt at simple agrarianism, the life of Neolithic hunter-gatherers, or even simple foraging. But it is of course the author herself who decides on the event and its stopping point, and the particular set of human capabilities whose staging they allow.

---

20. Schiller (1998) 228–29. Suvin (1979) 20 pairs science fiction and the pastoral idyll as worlds in which human relations in the present are subject to analogous forms of cognitive estrangement through temporal displacement.

21. Le Guin (2019) 707–708, citing Howard A. Norman's introduction to *The Wishing Bone Cycle*.

In *The Last Man*, Mary Shelley chose Greek agrarianism, but this is by no means the most popular stopping point for postapocalyptic fiction as a whole, which ranges from the medieval English city-state and its barbarian hinterlands to indigenous forms of life in precolonial California and the Siberian subarctic. Whatever form of life an author settles upon, her characters' efforts to attain sustenance and security are typically highlighted as the occupations most directly productive of satisfaction, and this immediate conjuncture of occupation and mentation is generally understood to be superior to the elaborate, reflective interiority of pre-apocalyptic civilization. My account of the return of the past in postapocalyptic fiction follows a rough periodization into *fin-de-siècle*, interwar, atomic, and contemporary fictions. It is not a comprehensive study along the lines of William Wagar's *Terminal Visions*. I concentrate on works that are intently focused on the intersection of occupation and mentation, and on staging what can be learned about human capabilities from a gleaning of Deep History.

Fin-de-siècle

Richard Jefferies's *After London, or Wild England* (1885) is set in a southland that has, through some unspecified apocalyptic event, reverted to a form of medievalism. The site of vanished London is now a toxic marsh. On the margins of the huge lake that occupies the center of England, city-states have arisen, while gypsies and nomadic pastoralists inhabit the backcountry. The novella tells the story of Felix Aquila, a disaffected junior member of the minor nobility, who escapes the claustrophobic limitations of his destined form of life. Abandoning the antiquarian ruminations to which he has devoted himself on his father's estate, he builds a boat and sets sail upon the lake. In the course of various adventures, he becomes a *voyageur*, a man at arms, a king's adviser, a wanderer in disgrace, and a victorious warlord.

Polis civilization is no better in *After London* than in Victorian London. Its medieval cities with their guilds and stratified social organization are just as stifling, and the activities on offer just as pointless and unsatisfying. But the wider world of *After London* is infinitely more rewarding. No one is surveying the hinterland, and Felix's occluded capabilities have free rein to develop. Like Delany's Blake, he learns how to navigate by the stars and live off the land. Self-realization is possible within the horizon of life and death, in a world that has dispensed with the shackles and safety nets of civilization. There is now an outside once again, and Felix is able to live the life of a maroon.

As Neil Roberts and Jimmy Casas Klausen have argued, marronage is a kind of perpetual exit strategy, continually enacted as motion toward the outside. The maroon's vocation is "to be permanently opposed to everything down below, the plain and the people enslaved to it." The maroon is inspired toward a liminal and transitional space in which to enact a form of life that is neither the bondage of the slave nor the liberty of the citizen. Unoccupied territory is fundamental to this freedom. Marronage is thetic in the way that poetry is thetic: it posits a space of freedom, and the maroon sets out to enact the freedoms this space affords.[22]

Felix's marronage requires a postapocalyptic Nature. Jefferies's loathing of Victorian neomedievalism is grounded in his understanding that medieval society was just as debilitating as his own. He frames this belief in Rousseauian terms: both forms of life entail a shearing of human capabilities to the point where "we can do nothing for ourselves."[23] The recovery of human capabilities

---

22. Roberts (2015) 4–15, 171; Klausen (2014) 226–28. Suvin (1983) 373–77, while praising many aspects of *After London*, misunderstands its conception of freedom as "individualist, escapist salvation" because the only kind of freedom he recognizes is "human collective freedom" in contrast to the determination of Nature.

23. Jefferies cited in Frost (2017) xviii–xix, who also observes that it is possible to think of Felix's encounter with the barbarian tribes outside the polis walls "in terms of encounters between indigenous peoples and European and American settlers" (xlvi). Sumpter (2011) 323–24 offers a detailed account of the ways in which "anthropological as well as historiographical understandings of barbarism" shape the portrayal of life among the extrapolis peoples of *After London*.

means leaving the polis behind. As Octavia Butler puts it, "The best way to do something else is to go someplace else where the demands on us will be different. Not because we are going to go someplace else and change ourselves, but because we will go someplace else and be forced to change."[24] Butler is thinking of off-planet space, but for Jefferies it is the space outside the polis that by his own time is already only recuperable with civilization's demise.

After London is genuinely postapocalyptic. Its strict entailment of marronage and self-realization can be better appreciated by comparison with the utopian fictions of William Morris, Edward Bellamy, and Samuel Butler. The first part of *After London* is entitled "The Relapse into Barbarism," and Morris admired its vision of "barbarism once more flooding the world."[25] His *News from Nowhere* is in many ways an imaginative response to Jefferies's novella. He imagines a world of Thames Valley micropolities without London looming over them as a megalopolis of cheap labor and degraded sociality. As one might expect, he is closely concerned with the relationship between occupation and mentation, but he does not stray far from the idea that satisfaction is easily discovered in the craft activities at which his own workshops excelled. His neomedievalism is a projection of what was best about Victorian England, if it could only take stock of where it was heading and make some salutary adjustments.

Morris begins with the regular call to arms of speculative anthropology—"You need to go back in order to go forward"—but there is no need to go very far back in order to make things right, and then you can start going forward again. His vision is as progressive as his rallying cry to the reader: "Go back again, now you have seen us. Go back and be happier for having seen us, for having added a little hope to your struggle."[26] *News from Nowhere*

---

24. Octavia Butler quoted in Francis (2010) 71.
25. Ebbatson (1977).
26. Morris (1993) xxvii, 228.

is closer in spirit to the calm, orderly utopias of work in Edward Bellamy's *Looking Backward* and Samuel Butler's *Erewhon* than it is to Jefferies's vision of London engulfed by a pestilential swamp, as illiterate feudal barons survey from the safety of their castles and walled cities a hinterland populated by roaming tribes of gypsies and semiferal bushmen.

Jefferies offers a vision of individual self-realization outside the polis walls. Felix becomes who he is by fleeing into a space that affords him opportunities to make use of his latent capabilities. The protagonists of *Looking Backward* and *Erewhon* forget who they were. In *Looking Backward*, "momentary obscuration of the sense of one's identity" has a double sense. On one hand, it is simply the physiological effect of time travel itself—arriving in the future entails a particularly severe form of jet lag. But it is also the form of selfhood that this future world has been able to achieve—the bracketing of individual self-realization at which its utopian community aims, and which the hero feels for himself as he enters this "Golden Age [that] lies before us and not behind us."[27] In *Erewhon*, the protagonist likewise suffers "dreadful doubt as to my own identity—as to the continuity of my past and present experience" at the threshold moment before he enters the novel's utopian community.[28] *After London*, by contrast, stages an intensification of selfhood; everything that being human could be is available again in the environment of marronage.

Adaptation in *After London* consists to a large degree in forgetting. The apocalyptic event is fabulized within the story world without authorial correction. It belongs to a past that is impossible to locate as distant or proximate—either to ourselves or to its characters—according to our own ways of reckoning with time. Sub- or postscientific fabulation exercises what passes for historical inquiry. With the loss of records has come a return of mythology and theology, which are barely distinguishable from each

---

27. Bellamy (2007) 45, 197.
28. Butler (1970) 65.

other and enacted as streams of competing pseudohistories about the world of the past and its demise. These accounts are polemical in tone and have the flavor of medieval disputation as they are voiced by the narrator, especially in his hostility to "Silvester," and his work upon the "Unknown Orb," a cosmic theory of the apocalypse as being due to the influence of a "dark body travelling in space."[29]

Technological understanding has likewise faded in *After London*. In this world, "The Romans and Greeks are more familiar to us than the men who rode in the iron chariots and mounted to the skies."[30] But whereas what passes for intellectual inquiry is obviously fabulous, the return of classical antiquity is as difficult to parse as it is in *The Last Man*. A yearly feast hosted by one of the novel's dynastic families features a performance of Sophocles' *Antigone*, since "in some undefinable manner the spirit of the ancient Greeks seemed . . . in accord with the times." Now that people "had or appeared to have so little control over their own lives," they admire how the Greeks staged the workings of fate, since they too "might well imagine themselves overruled by destiny." The reemergence of an inflexible caste system underwrites this admiration: "As men were born so they lived; they could not advance, and when this is the case the idea of Fate is always predominant."[31]

Mental life and material culture converge. Greek tragedy asserts itself with renewed conceptual vigor because it has an unrivaled capacity to disclose the form of life that is lived in the novel's present and because it is short enough to copy by hand. But who is this apocalypse for? Within the neomedieval polis of *After London*, there is only slavery, endurance, and the uselessness of the effort to rival the achievements of technological civilization. Beyond its islanded polities, the retreat of civilization opens up the possibility

29. Jefferies (2017) 14–15.
30. Jefferies (2017) 16.
31. Jefferies (2017) 93–94.

of escape, and new forms of life that are neither paradises of work nor fatalistic resignation to one's appointed task. In the indifference to the alternative between the liberty of the citizen and the bondage of the slave, an opposing drive emerges that takes Nature as the necessary horizon of freedom. Philhellenism and neomedievalism are set against each other, and with their mutual cancelation a third possibility appears, not in dialectical resolution but through sheer, unremitting negation: "We must begin again like the Caveman.... We must destroy the idea of our knowing anything."[32]

Raoul Vaneigem's *The Movement of the Free Spirit* offers a useful modern analogue for Jefferies's historical imagination in *After London*. As its subtitle indicates—*General Considerations and Firsthand Testimony Concerning Some Brief Flowerings of Life in the Middle Ages, the Renaissance and, Incidentally, Our Own Time*— Vaneigem imagines a potential for life having partially revealed itself in the Middle Ages without ever being fully realized in a historical form of life. There is something that remains to be lived in historical existence, which historical fiction can bring to light by imagining history against itself. Paul Kingsnorth's *The Wake* is an excellent contemporary example of what the convergence of postapocalyptic and historical fiction can achieve in this regard. In Kingsnorth's novel, an Anglo-Saxon culture in the process of being suppressed by England's Norman conquerors reveals itself to us as an alternative form of life that never came to a full flowering of its own possibilities.

The destruction of the metropolis in *After London* is a favorite theme of *fin-de-siècle* postapocalyptic fiction in England.[33] M. P. Shiel's *The Purple Cloud* (1901) is most lavish in its attention to detail, but it is focused on destruction alone. It is not concerned with imagining the new forms of life that might emerge if London

---

32. Jefferies cited in Frost (2017) xxi.
33. Cf. Parrinder (1995) for the full scope of speculative fiction from Mary Shelley to H. G. Wells.

were removed from its position as a command-and-control center over the surrounding countryside.

By contrast, J. D. Beresford's *Goslings* (1912) envisions a plague that wipes out almost all English men, while the majority of women survive. With the collapse of industrial food production, London's female population empties out toward the food-bearing capacity of its hinterlands. In the convergence of small-scale agricultural subsistence and sexual scarcity, Beresford, like Shelley, imagines a return of Greek mentation.

Goslings engages with classical antiquity in large part through the figure of Pan that exercised such fascination over the *fin-de-siècle* weird tale—Arthur Machen's *The Great God Pan* (1890) and Algernon Blackwood's magnum opus, *The Centaur* (1911), are the most significant examples, with Nathaniel Hawthorne's *The Marble Faun* (1860) an illustrious predecessor. In *Goslings*, cathexis to the Greeks through the figure of Pan is neither sexual nor pantheistic in the first instance. Rather, Pan emerges out of the conjuncture of female sexuality and male die-off.

In *The Last Man*, Nature is an unmotivated agent of the annihilation of humankind as a whole, but in *Goslings* men are an infestation of the earth that Nature abhors. There is "no god favorable to man, now that he was dying."[34] As in Arthur Conan Doyle's *The Poison Belt* and Jack London's *The Scarlet Plague*, the pestilence that destroys male human beings is not an accident but Nature deliberately cleansing her body of parasites, like a gardener killing bacteria on a fruit with disinfectant: he "dips it into the poison and they are gone."[35]

Shelley's Nature manifests itself to the survivors of *The Last Man* as the presence among them of the benevolent deities upon whom they depend. In *Goslings*, the cosmos as hygienic agent, which manifests itself as gods that will put an end to human reproductive futurity, cleaves more closely to Hesiod's *Works and Days*. And to Greek epic more generally: in the *Cypria*, one of the later

---

34. Beresford (2013) 208.
35. Doyle (2001) 26.

poems that fill in the gaps of backstory and cosmology in Homer's *Iliad*, the Trojan War is the outcome of Zeus's desire to drastically reduce the number of human beings who so overburden the Earth that she cries out to him for relief.

As the vegetal world rebounds from overcultivation in *Goslings*, the abject human survivors likewise suspect that Nature's reinvigoration signifies their own immediate demise: "Were the old gods coming back to witness the death of man, as they had witnessed its birth?" They stand at the threshold of one of humankind's periodic extinction events, and they internalize their precariousness as divine surveillance. They cling to their former habits and clothes, which make them "invisible to the earth-gods" and "hid them from their knowledge." By contrast with the "vigour and cleanliness of plant life," they hope they are too vile to attract divine attention "in their tumbled clothes and unsightly remains of forgotten fashion." They are "as much out of place" in their new world "as if they had been set down in ancient Greece."[36]

Beresford is pessimistic about the survivors' capacity to selectively assimilate the return of the gods. "I've seen the great God Pan," one of them reflects; "those sailors in the Ionian sea were misinformed. He's not dead." For "why should Pan die and Dionysus live?"[37] Whereas Shelley imagines small-scale agrarianism fostering a return of Greek mythology through a strict entailment of the affects of dependency, in *Goslings*, the empty spaces that open up with the disappearance of intensive agriculture foster new forms of mentation that work against social cohesion. The novel's emergent agrarian communities easily lose sight of the goals of shared labor and technological recovery. Their members drift toward solitary obsessions—with self-adornment, illicit food consumption, and sexual pleasure beyond the reach of community governance. The return of the gods means the return of all the gods, and the survivors exhibit singular forms of devotion. They

---

36. Beresford (2013) 207–208, 174.
37. Beresford (2013) 209.

express the correlation between die-off and mentation without knowing it for what it is.

Until the *homines ex machina* ending, when new men arrive from overseas to reboot the future, the survivors' express concern is to "preserve our knowledge and hand it on" in the hope that there may someday be human beings who are able to make use of it again.[38] As in Hesiod, postapocalyptic unpreparedness is figured in their struggles on the road. The protagonists leave London with an "abominable truck," stuffed with useless possessions from their former home. They push it up hills and drag it down slopes, an impediment to their physical progress and psychic adaption until they finally abandon it when they reach one of the agrarian communities in the backcountry.

The road and the cart are an inseparable pair. The road is the site of exposure and demands constant vigilance if the survivors are to elude the human predators who populate it. The cart is an icon of the fragility of all the road stood for, the precariousness of the human concerns that the civilization of the polis made possible. Because men return in significant numbers before the new agrarian communities attain a steady state, it is impossible to judge whether the emergent forms of postapocalyptic life will foster the occluded capabilities of their inhabitants or whether further stages of glissade are required before such flourishing is afforded by new forms of occupation. At the end of the novel, the survivor communities are in transition—no longer clinging to the past, but not yet sure of what else they are doing either.

Interwar

Edward Shanks's *The People of the Ruins* (1920) is a time-travel narrative. At the outset of a civil war that returns Britain to a world of medieval city-states and roaming barbarians—a world much like that of Jefferies's *After London*—a science experiment is

---

38. Beresford (2013) 161–62, 240.

interrupted by revolutionary insurgents. A witness has been invited to observe a radium ray's power to preserve organic life, but the ray is inadvertently turned on the observer moments before the building in which the experiment is taking place is destroyed in the revolutionary uproar. The observer lies unconscious in its basement, buried but unharmed, until he awakens in the future.

The narrative device is akin to that of Edward Bellamy's *Looking Backward*, but while Bellamy's novel remained a best seller in England even after the First World War, it is not obvious that Shanks means to satirize its techno-utopian futurism. Time travel has to be accomplished somehow if the present is to look back upon itself from the future. In any event, the world that Shanks's protagonist awakens to is the opposite of Bellamy's. Having failed to resolve the inequities of industrial capitalism as *Looking Backward* recommends, the world is wracked by workers' revolts, and England regresses to warring chiefdoms, including the one centered on London in which the protagonist finds himself.

The People of the Ruins deploys many of the iconic mythemes of postapocalyptic fiction: the road as lasting reminder of the fragility of large-scale civilization, "always mutely and strangely a witness to the presence of other men"; the melancholy archivist poring over the records of the past in the hope of reconstructing a coherent narrative history, a project that strikes his contemporaries as a pointless esoteric fancy; an authorial account of technological regression as "glissading," in which society collapses back through prior stages of civilization until it reaches a steady state. In Shanks's account, the eventual resting place is a matter of contingent local circumstances, not a reflection of basic human desires or capabilities. He compares the global situation to his protagonist's survival in the demolished laboratory:

> The old world had collapsed, and the falling roof had crushed and blotted out forever most of what he had thought perpetually established. And then, amazingly, the stones and timbers had not continued in their fall to utter ruin. They had found

their level and stayed, jammed together, perhaps, fortuitously, to make a lower and narrower vault, which still sufficed to shelter the improvident family of men. The human race had not perished, had not even been reduced to utter barbarism. Its glissade into the abyss had been arrested, and it remained on the ledge of ground where it had been thrown. So much was left. How much?[39]

Most technical know-how has perished simply by fading from the minds of the survivors because it is no longer useful in the world they now inhabit. Would-be dynasts are in a race against time to secure what knowledge they still possess, lest this too be forgotten. Jeremy Tuft, the visitor from the past, is seconded to one such project by the ruler of London, known as The Speaker, who has preserved some artillery weapons from destruction but is not able to make them fire. Jeremy's task is to make this relic technology operable against The Speaker's adversaries, in return for which he will be rewarded with marriage to The Speaker's daughter and a long-term position of power.

Jeremy's efforts are successful in his first battle, against the army of the North, but in the second, the forces of London are routed by the Welsh. Jeremy, The Speaker, and his daughter flee to Sussex, where they hide from search parties in the backcountry along Stane Street, the old Roman road that runs through the South Downs. A second destruction is visited on London at the hands of the invading troops. The ruins Jeremy has witnessed will be ruined again, and the Roman road becomes the figure of this second future, in which all that will remain of the past is the minimal record of risk and domination legible in the road itself:

> He had a vision of the world sinking further below the point from which in his youth he had seen it, still on a level with him. Cities would be burnt, bridges broken down, tall towers destroyed and all the wealth and learning of humanity would

39. Shanks (2012) 46, 69, 113.

shiver to a few shards and a little dust. The very place would be forgotten where once had stood the houses that he knew; and the roads he had walked with his friends would be as desolate and lonely as the Stane Street of the Romans.[40]

The tragedy in which Jeremy has played a part "seemed to take its place with the road and everything else in a fantasy of idle invention." Shanks's self-referential closing gesture extends to Jeremy too, who, "wonder and portent that he was, strange anachronism, unparalleled and reluctant ambassador from one age to the next," finishes the novel by conflating the transhistorical warning offered by the road with that of the novel itself. As the Roman road is an anachronistic prophet of the destruction to come within the world of the story, so Jeremy, the weird ambassador of postapocalyptic fantasy, steps out of his fictional costume to make sure that we readers take heed of his warning in the present. This story about the future will be a prediction about the return of the past, unless we act now to avert its prophecy.

The flight of Jeremy and his companions is the marronage of *After London* under erasure. In the hinterland where they might have rediscovered their latent capabilities, they find only pursuit and death. *The People of the Ruins* is postapocalyptic fiction at its bleakest. There is neither a civilization worth saving nor a worthwhile alternative to the misery of modernity.

No work of postapocalyptic fiction announces its project of staging the return of a past form of life more clearly than Cicely Hamilton's *Theodore Savage: A Story of the Past or the Future* (1922). Or at least its American title does. Its English title, *Lest Ye Die*, cleaves more closely to the relationship between technology loss and apocalyptic prophecy. "Lest Ye Die" is the injunction against the recovery of technology that the novel's survivor communities place upon their members in the aftermath of a war that has returned Europe to the Stone Age. Large swathes of the earth are

---

40. Shanks (2012) 234.

uninhabitable, because national governments dropped chemical defoliants on their own territories to discourage migration from the cities to the food-bearing hinterlands when their major urban centers were bombed—a technological update of Zeus's reduction of the human population in the *Cypria*. Following the use of this "poison-fire," a war of all against all for the remaining viable land ensued, which continued until "the human herd had reduced itself to the point at which the bare earth could support it."[41]

But this destruction is only the *mise-en-scène* of *Theodore Savage*, whose protagonist will recover the occluded capabilities latent in his prophetic name. In his postapocalyptic life, Theodore experiences the alternation between action that is satisfying because it involves the skillful use of the body in matters of life and death, and sustained inactivity during downtime that is not the boredom of a civilized being condemned to amuse itself with leisure time distractions. He embraces the tranquility that is the mentational partner of meaningful occupation: "When the weather made wandering or fishing impossible he would sit under shelter, with his hands on his knees, passive, unimpatient, hardly moving through long hours, while he waited for the rain to cease."[42]

Theodore comes to an understanding of the Golden Age as "a wondrous condition of yesterday," an understanding he shares with Dicaearchus that poetic fictions are preserved folk memories of the *ataraxia* (freedom from care) of prehistorical living conditions. The angry, self-important deity who has authored humanity's return to the Stone Age is in fact giving them a chance to begin again and to recover this contentment for themselves. The Pandora's box of technics that Theodore's generation opened all the way turns out in the long view to be a real gift in disguise.

Theodore survives to become the last living connection with the world of the past. As he witnesses the commonplace technology of his youth become the matter of a new mythology, he

---

41. Hamilton (2013) 84.
42. Hamilton (2013) 95.

experiences a historical revelation commensurate with his understanding of what has been returned to him in the way of capabilities with the return of the past. He realizes his own generation could never have grasped the real meaning of the stories they inherited. They misunderstood what they received as the fantasies of prescientific people, and it has taken the apocalyptic event to reveal them for what they really were—lived experience in figurative clothing:

> It was the new world that taught him that man invents nothing, is incapable of pure invention; that what seem his wildest, most fantastic imaginings are no more than ineffective, distorted attempts to set down a half-forgotten experience. What had once appeared prophecies he saw to be memories; the Day of Judgment, when the heavens should flame and men call upon the rocks to cover them, belonged to the past before it belonged to the future. The forecast of its terrors was possible only to a people that had known them as realities; a people troubled by a dim race memory of the conquest of the air and catastrophe hurled from the skies. So, at least, his children taught him to believe.[43]

Everything that has happened to Theodore's civilization must have happened before for human beings to have the mythology that they have, but it is part and parcel of humanity's repeated glissades that future generations cannot recognize it as historical memory that has been worked upon in order to instruct, persuade, or dazzle its future audiences into accepting a form of life that experience has taught is best for them. This is not necessarily cause for regret. Epistemic limitation is a condition of cognitive growth, for Hamilton insists time and time again that "we never know anything except through our own experience" and that "we grasp nothing save through ourselves and our relationship to it."[44]

---

43. Hamilton (2013) 168.
44. Hamilton (2013) 165, 179.

Theodore soon realizes that it is better to learn how to do something for yourself than to make your survival dependent on the knowhow of others. Depending on others means your own life is inherently precarious, which detracts from contentment by substituting anxiety for capability. But the lesson of autarky, that capability breeds contentment, also applies to cultural representations. The culture of Theodore's postapocalyptic people emerges directly from their own occupations. Its combination of epistemic limitation and explanatory power reenacts the postapocalyptic mythologies of antiquity in its concern with how best to live under conditions of imminent catastrophe.

For Hamilton, the return of the past in Theodore's postapocalyptic people is a culture of real understanding because it comes out of the work of survival. She contrasts its authentic cathexis to lived experience with the self-deluding culture that estranged Theodore's prewar generation from the life of the body and genuine self-understanding. In his former life, Theodore won the hand of his boss's daughter because of his exquisite taste in porcelain, his cultural formation masking the subjection of desire to social ambition even from himself. By contrast, the first of his postapocalyptic unions is based on the frank acknowledgment of mutual sexual need, and the second extends his understanding of "duties and natural needs" to the "intimate lore of fatherhood."[45]

Hamilton, founder of the Women Writers' Suffrage League, endorses this transition through an authorial doppelgänger. In his initial wanderings through the postapocalyptic landscape, Theodore encounters a former society author who on his deathbed offers a rueful reflection on his own production of literary porcelain:

> I spent a year once—a whole year—on a book about a woman who was finding out she didn't love her husband. She was well fed and housed, lived comfortably—and I wrote of her as if she

---

45. Hamilton (2013) 161–62.

were a tragedy. The work I put into it—the work and the thought! I tried to get what I called atmosphere.... And all the time there was this in us—this raw, red thing—and I never touched it, never guessed what we were without our habits.[46]

Whether Hamilton is thinking of *The Portrait of a Lady*, *Madame Bovary*, or the silver fork novel more generally, she sets herself against the society novel's Venn diagram of manners, marriage, and introspection. Her fictional novelist's lament reprises elements of H. G. Wells's indictment of Henry James's work as "tales of nothingness,"[47] taken up again in Amitav Ghosh's complaints about the tiny crucibles of nineteenth-century realist fiction.[48] The point about generic ambition could hardly be clearer. Only by projecting itself beyond the realist novel's reproduction of existing social forms can fiction have anything useful to offer in the way of criticizing those forms, and imagining a form of life better suited to the full range of human capabilities and desires.

In *Theodore Savage*, a more satisfying sexual politics depends on a return to conditions of natural need, and the honesty it enables, rather than conscious rethinking on the part of its characters. Mentation is a direct outcome of occupation, but for this very reason Hamilton is pessimistic about long-term gains. Humankind can only be happy by forgetting what it thinks it knows, but it is also doomed to progressively reinstall the civilization that the apocalyptic event temporarily removed for the good of all. Happiness is a short-term external alleviation of human

46. Hamilton (2013) 79–80.

47. The famous assessment, cited by Wagar (2004) 119, is too good not to repeat in full: "Having first made sure that he has scarcely anything left to express, he then sets to work to express it, with an industry, a wealth of intellectual stuff that dwarfs Newton. He spares no resource in the telling of his dead inventions.... It is leviathan retrieving pebbles. It is a magnificent but painful hippopotamus resolved at any cost, even at the cost of its dignity, upon picking up a pea which has got into a corner of its den. Most things, it insists, are beyond it, but it can, at any rate, modestly, and with an artistic singleness of mind, pick up that pea."

48. Ghosh (2017) 66–73.

beings' involuntary tendency to reenact the misapprehension of their own needs: "In all things man untraditional held blindly to the wrongs he had forgotten; instinctively, not knowing whither they led, he trod the paths that his fathers had trodden before him."[49]

Why this should be so is unknowable. The small-scale, egalitarian, subsistence community in which Theodore finds contentment and tranquility will in due course be supplanted by the return of aristocracy, a slave class, and a hereditary monarchy. Humankind's perennial conflict between freedom and security is in the long run always resolved in favor of the latter. This is Hamilton's answer to Rousseau's question in *The Discourse on Inequality* about how and why human beings could ever have been induced to give up the freedoms of his speculative Neolithic for the constraints of civilization.

These questions are frankly acknowledged as Rousseauian in J. Leslie Mitchell's two novels of speculative fiction, *Three Go Back* (1932) and *Gay Hunter* (1934).[50] Both are novels of time travel. In *Three Go Back*, the protagonists are transported backward to a speculative Neolithic in the past. In *Gay Hunter*, they are transported forward to a speculative Neolithic that has superseded modern European civilization in the wake of an undisclosed apocalyptic event. In *Three Go Back*, the time travelers encounter contented hunter-gatherers who are proof that "Rousseau was right," and Mitchell repeatedly cites Percy Shelley's translation of Virgil's fourth eclogue to indicate that the novel's vision of a Golden Age which might one day return is continuous with the classical tradition that understands pastoral poetry to preserve folk memories of pre-agricultural life in figurative disguise.[51]

---

49. Hamilton (2013) 181.

50. Mitchell is the pen name used by Lewis Grassic Gibbon for his works of speculative fiction. He is better known for his novels of rural Scottish life, especially the trilogy *A Scots Quair*.

51. Mitchell (1999) 90, 102, 116, 121, 131–32.

In *Three Go Back*, the time travelers have an opportunity to change the course of history so that the fatal invention of agriculture and sedentary civilization never takes place. Sorely tempted as they are, they opt in the end to forgo this opportunity, trusting instead that human beings in the future will be able to access corporeal echoes of the experiences of their hunter-gatherer ancestors. These memories will function, as they always have, as "ghosts of a sanity that haunted mankind," even when this sanity appears to be irrecoverably disconnected from its origin in lived experience. It is a Rousseauian hope that rests upon faith in the body as a carrier of transhistorical experience and the belief that human beings can recover its abrogated capabilities by returning to the occupations of Deep History.

An adumbration of what this recovery would feel like is always available to human beings in the way they respond to the macrophenomena of Nature: "The sun and the wind, the splendours of simple things, had been theirs; theirs that Golden Age that was to live for ever."[52] Being with these phenomena is a trigger for the apprehension of lost capabilities and a foretaste of what a fuller participation in shared life with living beings as a whole would feel like. By virtue of their sojourn in the past, the time travelers retain this knowledge as conscious understanding, and they set out to unmake the industrial civilization they return to from within, before it dissolves in catastrophic self-destruction.

We should not be optimistic about their chances of success. One of the time travelers gives a Daoist inflection to the idea that goodness is only possible when it is not conscious pursuit of the good. He cites Lao-Tze, "writing of a Golden Age which has been considered mythical," but which yet "describes in vivid detail the character and conduct of those Old Stone Age primitives among whom I lived." He conflates this Golden Age with both the speculative Neolithic he visited and the Golden Age of the Greeks that is retained only in poetry's refracted annals: "They loved one

---

52. Mitchell (1999) 132.

another without knowing that to do so was benevolence.... Therefore their actions left no trace and there was no record of their affairs."[53] The belief that what is best for human beings is only attainable on the condition that it is not projected as a goal offers little platform for political action. For all the time travelers' efforts, the best hope for a return to the speculative Neolithic is the very catastrophe they seek to avert, and *Gay Hunter* is in fact set in the aftermath of the catastrophe anticipated in *Three Go Back*.

In *Gay Hunter*, a young American archaeologist of that name vacationing in the downlands of southern England is projected into a future in which reemergent hunter-gatherers have repossessed the landscape in which she arrived. Unworkable relics of industrial civilization persist, but the power supplies on which they depend are failing, and one of the novel's most compelling fantasies is an automated voice that seeks to perpetuate the memory of technics in the absence of a human population that can act upon its message. Faced with an insurrection of the Sub-Men they enslaved, the Hierarchs of technological civilization fashioned a machine that obsessively recalls their achievements. Mitchell's brilliant revisioning of Hesiod's strongly voiced postapocalyptic reminders that to be human is to be technological as a parasitic, self-replicating meme that would install itself in the human psyche, hijacking its capacity for communication:

> Now the whispering Voice was a blur of technicalities of which she [Gay Hunter] could make nothing—it was whispering at a gabble innumerable formulae and recipes it believed of supreme importance for members of the Hierarchies to know should they survive the debacle.[54]

In *Theodore Savage*, Cicely Hamilton claims that in the realm of technics, "what we think we own—owns us,"[55] a familiar position

---

53. Mitchell (1999) 120.
54. Mitchell (1989) 87.
55. Hamilton (2013) 81.

for the critique of technics, but compellingly realized in *Gay Hunter* as the desperation of last men who devote their final energies to the construction of a machine that will perpetuate the very forces that have wrought the destruction of their own best human capabilities. The counterpart of the Hierarchs' Voice are the Singers, the bards and storytellers who pass down the folk memories in which an understanding of the superiority of their own post-technological form of life is preserved.

In contrast to the detailed didacticism of the Hierarchs, the mode of access to these memories, and what gives them their persuasive authority, is imaginative assent to the experiences they afford. The way of knowing—the poeticism to which song is a portal—is set against complex forms of interiority that require discursive articulation. *Gay Hunter* contains an explicit critique of Freud for mistaking the form of life of defective human beings in local historical conditions for universal human experiences, and his concomitant emphasis on narrativized dreamwork as compensation for and reconstitution of displaced desires. The novel's hunter-gatherers dream seldom or never, because what they do all day is satisfying in itself: "They did not dream of life—they lived it and sang it instead."[56]

Like *Theodore Savage*, *Gay Hunter* has an answer to the question of whether human beings are doomed to recapitulate the civilization that the apocalyptic event removed and, if so, why. Even in the new Arcadia of a rewilded southern England, there are those who "still dragged ghostly fetters from the past—though they knew them not as fetters: probably saw them instead as guiding links to freedom and the full and unpained life." The "ghostly fetters" are resupplied by the shadow self of security that is inevitably called into being by a life lived within the immediate horizon of life and death. For all the satisfactions this life affords at the level of bodily capabilities, it also generates the thought of doing away

---

56. Mitchell (1989) 179.

with danger, and it is against this thought that human beings must contend if they are to persist in contentment.

Gay Hunter's time-travel companions attempt to capitalize on the projections of this shadow self. They determine to restore technological civilization by becoming masters of those among the hunter-gatherer population who unknowingly nurture within themselves this "seed of desire for safety, security" that everyone carries, whereas Gay herself knows that the fruit of this seed will "poison the minds of men" and "set them to climbing the bitter tracks to civilisation's bloody plateau."[57] As in *Three Go Back*, outcomes are only hinted at, but there is a strong suggestion that the best humankind can hope for in the long run is a rotation of crops, as one set of seeds, flowers, and fruits succeeds another in a never-ending cycle.

Atomic

Like *Three Go Back*, *Gay Hunter* is agnostic about the futures it imagines. At the end of the novel, Gay herself is returned to the present with conscious understanding of the superiority of the form of life she has experienced, and filled with hope that she may direct people toward it by persuading them of its virtues. She is an archaeologist who specializes in the city-states of the Maya, and both her novel and *Three Go Back* contain long historical excursuses on the life of the early humans they attempt to bring to life as fiction. The superiority claimed for the life of mobile pre-agrarian bands in comparison to that of sedentary agriculturalists rests upon a detailed consideration of what such people do all day. Mitchell's admiration for the occupations of flexible, opportunistic, nonspecialized generalists, in contrast to the repetitive and relatively unskilled tasks of large-scale cultivators, is, broadly speaking, in keeping with the position of contemporary anthropologists.[58]

57. Mitchell (1989) 114.
58. See, for example, Scott (2017) 59, 89–90.

Such detailed attention to the archaeological record is lacking in postwar British apocalyptic fiction. John Christopher's *The Death of Grass* (1956) deploys many of the structuring narrative tropes of the genre to great effect in its vision of survival in a world without agriculture—the return of the gods, the Golden Age, the conversion of technology to legend, the road as marker of civilization and narrative time—but the novel lacks the anthropological horizon of its predecessors.[59] Likewise, in Doris Lessing's *The Memoirs of a Survivor* (1974), the young people of its postapocalyptic world remake themselves into "tribes" as the "new social unit," but this form of life is compared to dogs going feral without the maroon understanding of rewilding. The perspective on social transformation comes from within the decaying civilization, and emergent forms of social organization are not plotted against the archaeological or anthropological record in detail. Indeed, it is suggested that such efforts belong to the wrongheaded book culture of the past. The novel dwells in some detail on the fortunes of an indigent family, the Ryans, whose existence was the subject of sociological study before the apocalyptic event: "A young man just out of university, whose aunt was a welfare worker on the case, had collected notes for a book, *The Barbarians We Make*, comparing the Ryans to those who pulled Rome down from its heights." The attempt to conceptualize contemporary existence in terms of past forms of life is naïve and unrevealing, and the novel's protagonist does not make any such efforts herself, beyond the occasional superficial remark about tribalism and animality: "Their packs and tribes had structure, like those of primitive man or of animals, where in fact a strict order prevails."[60]

So, too, in Denis Johnson's *Fiskadoro* (1985), which begins with an epigraph from Victor Turner, it is asserted that "the story of the world is happening again," but it is difficult to trace the logic of reversion in the form of life of the survivors on the Florida Keys,

59. Christopher (2016) 72, 111, 140, 119, 160.
60. Lessing (1974) 34–35, 103, 171.

which embraces reverence for an unexploded nuclear weapon, tribal Islam, and the practice of subincision.[61] There is neither a structuring text for these beliefs, as in Walter M. Miller's *A Canticle for Leibowitz* (1960), in which bookleggers and memorizers shape the conception of a Hesiodic succession of ages in the aftermath of atomic warfare, nor any obvious relationship between occupation and mentation in the life of the survivors, who eat fish, clean fish, cook fish, then eat fish again in an endlessly recurring cycle, without these basic practices of survival appearing to inflect their beliefs in any legible fashion.

This absence is equally pronounced in Nevil Shute's *On the Beach* (1957). A postnuclear novel set in Australia evinces no interest in the continent's indigenous people, and this indifference contributes significantly to the unrelenting listlessness with which its colonial people await their fate. Faced with the end of their own form of life, they are resolutely incapable of imagining an alternative. While the novel is set up to preclude a future—a radioactive cloud from a nuclear war in the Global North drifts slowly southward, eliminating all zoological life in its path with absolute predictability, like a train that always arrives on time—it is of course the author who determines the possibilities for postapocalyptic life. Without the perspective of other cultures, there is no future worth imagining. As the novel contemplates the total extinction of humankind, there is nothing to hope for and nothing to regret, and its version of postapocalyptic life is limited to the repression strategies of midlevel administrators who, with their own deaths in plain sight, are too timid to transgress even local sexual mores. If there is such a thing as the silver-plated fork novel, this is what it looks like. Its one suggestion is that the newspapers might have behaved better in the lead-up to the nuclear conflagration, but that's all it has to offer in the way of speculative futures. There is not a single indigenous person in the book, not a moment of reflection on how these inhabitants of Australia might feel about the

---

61. Johnson (1985) 165, 158, 180–85.

apocalypse that has been visited upon them, or how the colonials might have imagined a different future with their forms of life in mind.

The anthropological horizon remains insistently present in Pat Frank's *Alas, Babylon* (1959). Frank's novel imagines a country whose urban centers have been obliterated by atomic weapons. The story centers on the town of Fort Repose, Florida, which has been spared the destruction of the nearby cities, either by oversight or because its location and population are insignificant in the global conflict. The town is guided toward a steady state of small-scale agrarian subsistence by Randy Bragg, a descendant of its founding father, who settled the land after serving as an army officer in the Seminole Wars. Randy is aided in this task by the Henrys, descendants of his ancestor's slaves, who continue to farm an adjacent property that they now own.

Alas, Babylon features many of the regular mythemes of postapocalyptic fiction: highways that have becomes sites of exposure populated by criminal vagrants; new forms of occupation that prove to be more satisfying to the survivors than what they did before; a first glissade to the life of one hundred years ago, which eventually bottoms out at the life of four thousand years ago; the formation of a community based on "common needs"; the struggle to enact leadership and martial law when faced with murderous intruders.[62] The Henrys partially occupy the niche of indigenous knowledge. They know how to raise their own food, they run their own water lines from the river, and they are the first to fashion hunting spears when ammunition for guns runs out, marking "North American civilization's return to the Neolithic Age."[63] And yet the emergent community's precarious survival is guaranteed only through recourse to the anthropological record as such. Eventually all the salt in the town's stores is consumed. Fort Repose is inland, and it is only when Randy remembers that the

---

62. Frank (2005) 100–101, 111, 154, 253, 120, 163, 137, 194–95.
63. Frank (2005) 185.

founding father's journal contains an account of how the Seminoles got salt from a mineral pool that the crisis is averted.

Alas, Babylon enacts an awkward compromise with the anthropological record. On one hand, indigenous knowledge is the key to survival. On the other, the life it permits to continue is settler colonial in form: small-scale agrarianism from which slavery has been eliminated but in which the paternalism of the founders works out best for everyone in the long run—a chastened, more self-aware version of the original project. George R. Stewart's *Earth Abides* (1949) is more radical. Set in the Bay Area in the aftermath of a global pandemic that wipes out the vast majority of the human population, it imagines a thoroughgoing reversion to tribalism. The protagonist of this "ultimate Robinson Crusoe tale" is called Ish. His name invokes Ishi, the last of the Californian Yahi people, who famously lived on as a guest of Ursula Le Guin's anthropologist father, Alfred Kroeber, on the Berkeley campus— where parts of *Earth Abides* are set and where Stewart taught in the English department—and also Melville's Ishmael, the only survivor of the *Pequod*, fictional microcosm of modern American slaughterhouse efficiency.

The narrative arc of *Earth Abides*, in which Ish outlives all other survivors of the apocalyptic event to become "the last American," is plotted as industrial civilization's self-cannibalism en route to the recovery of new forms of life: "The world of those Indians passed away.... And now our world that followed theirs has passed, too."[64] To survive the passing, Ish relies on his skills as a "moderately practical though not mechanical camper." He is unconscious for the apocalyptic event itself because he is bitten by a poisonous snake while away from home on a camping trip. His first response to the postapocalyptic world in which he awakens is to set off on a sightseeing tour, a "see America first" version of the lone-survivor Grand Tours of *The Last Man* and *The Purple Cloud*. On this tour, he encounters regional forms of survivalism

64. Stewart (2006) 28.

that will eventually give rise to entirely disparate culture zones, as small groups of survivors come together to fashion response strategies that combine their own creative "culturecraft" with the determinism of what the local land and ecology allow.[65]

On his return, Ish visits the library, where he finds Robinson Crusoe's religious preoccupations "boring and rather silly," and wonders whether Defoe's hero really wanted to be rescued from his island "where he was lord of all that he surveyed." He concludes that he himself is afraid of human entanglements but is nonetheless drawn into human community by sexual need and a friendly dog belonging to a local female survivor—convergent centers of attraction whose powers are restaged and separately analyzed by Robert Matheson in *I Am Legend*. These first acts of companionship lead to the formation of a survivor group centered on his parents' old neighborhood. Others join the nuclear couple and their pet, and they call themselves "The Tribe," as Ish recapitulates for them the "story of mankind" with books of anthropology, history, and the philosophy of history from the Berkeley library. They come to appreciate the satisfactions of their new life, and they record the passing of each year with a name agreed upon by the group.[66]

The book's second part is introduced with an epigraph from Crèvecoeur about the superiority of social life among the American Indians compared to that of the European settlers. It is the theme of the frontispiece of Rousseau's *Discourse on Inequality*: while there are countless defectors from the colonial settlements, no indigenous person chooses to remain with the colonials when given a chance to return to their own people. The epigraph marks a tipping point in the narrative of *Earth Abides*. As the children born after the apocalyptic event begin to outnumber the survivors and the latter continue to die off, The Tribe increasingly shed

---

65. I borrow the term "culturecraft" from the discussion of projects of real-world survivalism in Mitchell (2002). I explore Mitchell's concept in detail in the analysis of survivalist fiction in chapter 3.

66. Stewart (2006) 38, 84, 99, 141.

whatever vestiges of civilization they had retained. They forget about marking the years and doing the handicrafts that Ish thought would be good for them as "creative outlets."[67] He recognizes that their present form of life affords more immediate satisfactions and does not insist on the compensations that culture once offered to human beings when they were shorn of their more fundamental capabilities.

Earth Abides pushes the anthropological horizon down from the level of authorial commentary to characterological self-fashioning. The anthropology Ish learns at the library is adaptive for the ways in which he shapes, or refrains from shaping, the life of The Tribe. He recognizes that cultures in crisis, like the Plains Indians of the nineteenth century, whose "traditional way of life had rudely been made impossible," might not be the best models with which to grasp what is slowly unfolding around him. He is something of an ideal reader of anthropology, both sympathetic and critically insightful. He recognizes, for example, that in the anthropological horizon of Deep History, work and play were not set against each other but were complementary occupations in a single form of life. Hunting, gathering, and nursing were not opposed to singing, dancing, and sex, as needs were opposed to desires in the culture in which he was raised, and he can see that the speculative Neolithic that has grown up around him is such a form of life again. There are "not even the words" now with which to set desire against need.[68]

The postapocalyptic children of *Earth Abides* know where to find streams when the reservoir system breaks down and piped water gives out, whereas the adults of the Old Times are "tied to street maps." Using this environmental know-how is no more a task to them than going on a trip, shooting with a bow, or "bull dodging," the new local sport. They like music but prefer playing to listening, which remains the marker of the supplanted

---

67. Stewart (2006) 142.
68. Stewart (2006) 167, 193.

civilization in *Alas, Babylon* and *I Am Legend*. "Choctaw-like imperturbability" is the new social affect.

Ish's relation to the past is eventually reduced to the hammer he carries with him at all times, which the youth view as a magical artifact proper to him alone. It is a form of *mana*, he reflects, as he himself is becoming a god, an object of reverence, but also of mild ill-treatment when he fails to deliver the desired response to the young people who seek his oracular guidance. He tries to imagine how what has befallen him might look to an anthropologist from thousands of years in the future, and he comes to an understanding of the Golden Age mythology of the past as folk memories of the happier existence that preceded large-scale civilization, the fateful moment when human beings exchanged the "free wandering life" of hunter-gatherers for the "security (and drudgery)" of agriculture and the domestication of animals.[69]

Ish's preservation as a living remainder of technological civilization is much like the fate of Cicely Hamilton's Theodore Savage, and Ish answers Rousseau's question about the exchange of freedom for security in much the same way as his predecessor: "They had not willed it, but it ruled them all. And so by a thousand little surreptitious paths they tried to escape." But Stewart is more sanguine than Hamilton about the young people's chances of retaining the freedoms they have been gifted by the apocalyptic event. There is no suggestion that they are doomed to follow in the tracks of their forgotten ancestors or that forgetting these ancestors will inevitably draw them into harm's way. At the end of the novel, the youth are fully other with respect to Ish, who can only admire their passage into an unforeseeable future. They look like they have attained a steady-state post-glissade life, but the predictive powers of the anthropological record are exhausted with their return to tribalism and their recovery of the form of the social bond that Crèvecoeur calls "singularly captivating."[70]

---

69. Stewart (2006) 177, 204, 220–21, 284, 312–13.
70. Stewart (2006) 294.

Is it better to arrest the glissade or let it run its course? *Alas, Babylon* comes down firmly on one side of this question and *Earth Abides* just as firmly on the other. David Brin's *The Postman* (1985) revisits the issue via a minor interaction in Pat Frank's *Alas, Babylon*. Faced with the collapse of the national banking system, the manager of the Fort Repose bank is pleased to note the arrival of the local mail carrier and quotes to him the unofficial motto of the U.S. Postal Service: "Neither rain nor snow nor dark of night . . ."[71] To which the mail carrier responds: "This is my last delivery."[72] Not all that much is at stake in this interaction for Frank. The mail carrier is eager to get back to his family, the bank manager is a coward whose identity depends on minor forms of *amour-propre*, and the mail system, like the banking system, is down and out. Their encounter is a minor incident in the return of the past, but from this minor incident Brin develops an insightful counternarrative of the performative basis of civilization's social bond.

In *The Postman*, a postapocalyptic traveler makes his living as a wandering player, journeying from settlement to settlement, where he performs what he can remember of Shakespeare and other highlights of the vanished civilization. While on his travels, he is set upon by highwaymen and flees into the woods, where he finds an abandoned Post Office jeep, with its mail carrier dead inside it. The mail carrier died in the performance of his duties against all odds. He, and those whose letters he bore, "tried this hard to keep the light alive."[73] The actor takes his clothes and boots because his own have been stolen, but he soon comes to enact the figure of the postman for the communities he visits, instantiating

---

71. The motto has no official standing and is, interestingly, an adaptation of the ancient Greek historian Herodotus's account of the courier system of the Persian Empire (*Histories* 8.98), the most extensive civilization of his time. See https://about.usps.com/who-we-are/postal-history/mission-motto.pdf. Tracking the inevitable collapse of such hubristic global empires is a staple of Greek and Roman historiography.

72. Frank (2005) 97.

73. Brin (1985) 32.

for them the possibility that through collective belief they might bring the lost America back into being.

What stands in the way of the success of this collective performance is the return of previous forms of historical life that block out the belief that imaginative possibilities can have direct social outcomes. Scarcity has led to crop-indebtedness and sharecropping. Further stages of glissade are in evidence too as barbarian survivalists beyond the stockades of the remaining micropolities raid the settlements for women, food, and slaves. The return to subsistence lends an aura of inevitability, not just to what people do all day, but to the relationship between occupation and mentation. When mere existence is so precarious, speculation seems not merely a pointless distraction but counterindicated as a survival strategy. As in *After London*, the glissade is not merely technological but entails general societal resignation to what passes for fate. The form of life that prevails is the form of life that must be.

And yet the predicament in which people find themselves is in fact a direct consequence of partisan deployment of the historical record. At the heart of the calamitous social conflicts that wrack postapocalyptic America are the writings of Nathan Holn, in whose historical fantasies Aaron Burr would have led an American Empire to global domination had Alexander Hamilton not undermined this project with his own vision of an America of ethnic inclusiveness. Holn's writings inspire "armed and armored" white males to take back America for themselves, and Brin devotes two full pages to a lengthy citation from Holn's work of alternative history, *Lost Empire*.[74] The past has new imaginative agency in a situation of unprecedented historical fluidity, and the lengthy citation stages its power to radicalize and convert.

Against alternative history's power of conversion, Brin sets theater's collective will to believe, not just in the person of his protagonist, but in the female insurgents who are inspired to act by the example of Greek drama. An imaginative mashup of

74. Brin (1985) 252–53.

Aristophanes' comic Lysistrata and Aeschylus's tragic Danaids becomes an antisurvivalist call to arms for the women of the settlements. They engage in suicide terrorism, infiltrating the Holnist compounds as concubines and killing their captors when an opportunity presents itself.

Ensuring the survival of the good by shouldering the responsibility for capital punishment is a regular crisis point for the emergent communities of postapocalyptic fiction. In *Alas, Babylon*, Randy sentences highwaymen to death by hanging, and in *Earth Abides*, The Tribe execute the interloper Charlie, who threatens the reproductive health of the community: "The all-necessary State had arisen, with death in its hands," Ish frets.[75] *The Postman* tweaks this mytheme with the idea that it is women who must assume the responsibility to "cull" irredeemable males.[76] It is likewise distinctive of *The Postman* that it is drama, Rousseau's *bête noire*, that is the imaginative agent in this assumption of responsibility. In Brin's world, civilization is a shared performative endeavor, enabled by willing suspension of disbelief on the part of the actors who are also its audience. Solitary survivalists perish in their bunkers in the early days of postapocalyptic struggle, without having had the chance to live their dream of a more satisfying, more authentic, primitivist form of life. The battle for the future of humankind is waged between two versions of civilization that are collective fantasies, more or less knowingly entertained as such, with the help, in the end, of a late-model cyborg soldier named Powhatan, who has been engineered to remain loyal to the biological humans who made him. The recovery of primordial species capabilities has no place in Brin's novel. Satisfaction is the realization in lived experience of what began as imaginative self-projection. There is no deep self to be recovered, only a future self to be attained if civilization can be rebooted more circumspectly, more or less at the point where it left off.

75. Stewart (2006) 279.
76. Brin (1985) 193, 226, 312.

Contemporary

Jean Hegland's *Into the Forest* (1996) includes *The University of California Publications in American Archeology and Ethnology* and *The Way We Lived: California Indian Reminiscences* among its acknowledgments. The story that follows, of two sisters coping with the aftermath of an undesignated apocalyptic event, is thus explicitly framed from the outset within the horizon of speculative anthropology. Nell and Eva are introduced as sibling Crusoes, surviving like "shipwrecked orphans" after their mother dies of illness and their father is killed in a chainsaw accident, leaving them alone in the backwoods of northern California, where they are dependent for the immediate future on supplies of canned food and dry goods their father stockpiled.[77]

The sisters have two major decisions to face in the early days of their isolation. Nell's boyfriend is fashioning a vehicle with which to undertake the long journey east with a group of his friends and family, to seek out whatever may remain of the United States government. Nell is initially tempted, but Eva is already attuned to the Hesiodic register of postapocalyptic transportation and won't be drawn into a discussion of "what sort of wheels would work best for the handcart."[78] Nell too eventually comes to think better of the road and decides to remain behind with her sister.

Nell and Eva's home site feels like a place of pastoral seclusion, but Eva is raped by an intruder, and the sisters must decide whether to continue living in their cabin, whose security is an illusion, or to trust themselves to the woods. They have a primitive shelter in a hollowed-out redwood stump they used to play in as children, which Nell has modified for use as a storage bin for acorns and a blind for hunting wild pigs. They burn down the cabin and retreat to the woods with Eva's baby. From the cabin's extensive library, Nell saves only *Native Plants of Northern*

---

77. Hegland (1998) 2.
78. Hegland (1998) 130.

California, which they found "wedged between *Madame Bovary* and a book about the Spanish Civil War," a book of Pomo Indian stories for the infant they have named Burl, and the index of the family encyclopedia, the "master list of all that had once been made or told or understood."[79]

Into the Forest reverses the poles of security and freedom that structure the relationship between civilization and the return to the past in postapocalyptic fiction. The sisters realize they are not risking anything by taking to the woods. Just the opposite, in fact. It is inside the cabin that they feel "both exposed and trapped," whereas the forest offers both security and freedom, nurturing their new form of life in the manner of a nurse log:

> Even when redwoods are toppled or otherwise injured, they have a remarkable adaptation for survival. Wartlike growths of dormant buds called burls are stimulated to produce sprouts which grow from a fallen or damaged tree. It is common to see young trees formed from burls encircling an injured parent tree.[80]

Neither the sisters nor their author is naïve about what this form of life entails. Nell works hard to master the process that makes acorns edible by leaching tannic acid out of them, which she has read about in her parents' books about the area's indigenous inhabitants, and it is in light of this course of study, both intellectual and practical, that she comes to reject her first vision of postapocalyptic life, a horse-and-cart world of short-term making do "while we were waiting for the life we had known to start back up again." This vision of a world getting by on old-timey bricolage was, she realizes, an extrapolation of her father's predilections, just as the journey across America was Eli's young man's vision quest. She must instead come up with a future that is her own but also shareable with her sister and her sister's baby. Finding out what the

---

79. Hegland (1998) 173, 239.
80. Hegland (1998) 146, 168.

Indians ate, she asks herself how she could have spent her whole life on their home site and know so little about them. She must now "learn a new language without the help of tapes and books, a language for which there are no longer any native speakers."[81]

Like Randy's people in *Alas, Babylon*, Nell and Eva are saved by dead Indians, but only by embracing their knowledge as best they can as the only way to survive in the landscape. There are no settler-colonialist half-measures in *Into the Forest*. If it is true that "for at least ten thousand years before the arrival of the Spaniards, the Pomo enjoyed a rigorous but relatively peaceful life" in the forest, this life will only be theirs by destroying the alternatives, so that a new form of life can emerge in the opening this destruction has made. Eventually, this opening will become ontological. Nell will come to see herself as "just a human, another creature" in the midst of the forest. But as in *The Postman*, the initial push comes from an act of historical imagination. It is by "reading the words of the people who inhabited the forest before us" that she and her sister are able to inhabit it. The way to ontological culturecraft is opened by an initial exposure to indigenous history as it is gleaned from the pages of a book.[82]

In due course, Eva and Nell are visited by the protective spirit of the forest in the form of a bear, but this possibility is not something they could have fashioned for themselves, from their own words alone. It is only by allowing themselves to be inhabited by their predecessors that this spirit can reach them, and this inhabitation is enabled by their occupations: "Although we constructed logical arguments and elaborate justifications, I don't think it was logic that finally persuaded us, but the fact that it felt good to be out in the woods, gathering acorns, drying berries, drinking our wild teas, and cooking our meals by the daytime fire Eva kindled in the fire pit we built just outside the door of the stump." Occupation is prior to mentation, and when Nell dreams of the bear eating

---

81. Hegland (1998) 189, 78–79, 172–73.
82. Hegland (1998) 177–78.

her head, it is because the forest has already eaten the head she had: "When it lifts its mouth from my empty shoulders, I can see the world as well as ever—in fact, things have a lucidity I had never before imagined, and I think, *What an effort it was to have to lug my head around with me for so long.*"[83]

What remains for Nell and Eva is the *ataraxia* (freedom from care) of reattunement to the forest and its moods:

> I fixed a stew of acorn mush and dried blackberries for breakfast yesterday morning. As I stirred the pot I remembered the berries drying in the late summer heat, the drone of flies and bees, the beads of blood on my arms from the brambles, the indelible juices on my fingers. I remembered the long days of gathering acorns, hour after hour of bending and crawling, until my back felt permanently stooped, my hands had been pricked by a million brittle oak leaves, and when I closed my eyes, I saw a sea of acorns.
>
> The steam was warm and fragrant in the chill air. I was hungry and I could feel my stomach clenching like another strong muscle. But just as I was lifting the first spoonful to my mouth, I heard a voice say Wait.
>
> For a wild moment I thought, Mother. I even stood to meet her, but outside the stump I saw only the familiar forest, heard only the incessant drip of rain. I breathed the moist, green-tinged air, and then, on an impulse I never tried to understand, I took the mush-pot and walked around the stump, pausing four times to spoon a pile of steaming food onto the wet earth.
>
> I stoked my fire, sat cross-legged just inside the stump, watching the rain drip through the forest. My stomach felt tight and small, my lungs big and loose. My hands were quiet in my lap. I felt as if I were waiting, though I had no idea why, or for what. At times thoughts came to me—I should gather more wood, I should check the roof to see how it's holding out, I

---

83. Hegland (1998) 189–93.

should move the water bucket out into the rain, but they lacked force, remained ideas as passive—and passing—as the sky is grey, the rain is falling, I can feel the weight of my shirt on my back.

I was still sitting like that when darkness took the forest. The air thickened, the sky deepened, the woods closed in around me, until at last I could see only the final coals of my untended fire glowing like a heart's secrets. I had to fight an impulse, the first real impulse I had had since I spooned my breakfast on the earth, to pluck one of those red jewels from its bed of ashes and pop it in my mouth.

Even more gradual than the fade of the sun's light was the fade of that handful of coals, but finally they, too, were gone, so slowly that even though they had my whole attention I could never say when they were extinguished, leaving me in the absolute darkness of a moonless rainy night, until the coal inside me was the only fire left.

In the blackness just beyond me, the rain kept falling, masking whatever other noises those woods might contain. I sat emptied before the dead fire, watching the darkness. My face felt as though it were wrapped in velvet, and it seemed my cheeks and forehead had grown a thousand new eyes, though they, too, saw only blackness. After a time, I drowsed, still sitting cross-legged, my hands still lax in my lap.[84]

I cite this passage at such length because it stages so compellingly the final link in the feedback loop between autarky and cosmic contentment that Rousseau completes in *Reveries of the Solitary Walker*. The zero-sum game between the sentiment of existence and the judgment of others structures Rousseau's speculative reconstruction of Deep History, from the claim in *The Discourse on Inequality* that "man's first sentiment was that of his existence,"[85] to the discovery in the *Reveries* that withdrawal from

---

84. Hegland (1998) 229.
85. Rousseau (1997) 161.

social life allows an efflorescence of this sentiment in ways he would not have previously thought possible. In *The Discourse on Inequality*, this feeling remains at the very horizon of the possibilities that his poeticism is trying to reach: "How are we to imagine the sort of pleasure that a savage takes in spending his life alone in the depths of forests?" But in his island life on Lake Bienne, he becomes autarkic, "self-sufficient like God." He grows accustomed to the daily relationship between self-loss and the feeling of existence that comes from a life directed to the satisfaction of natural needs and the contemplative platform such limitation affords:

> The feeling of existence unmixed with any other emotion is in itself a precious feeling of peace and contentment which would be enough to make this mode of being loved and cherished by anyone who could guard against all the earthly and sensual influences that are constantly distracting us from it in this life and troubling the joy it could give us.[86]

Autarky and connectivity are a virtuous circle. Self-sufficiency enables a self that has allowed its immediate delight in the feeling of existence to be replaced by the anxious pleasure that waits on the judgment of other human beings to reconnect with living beings as a whole. Speculative anthropology is enacted along this axis of connectivity to living beings as a whole, for it is here that the abrogation of the sentiment of existence in the social life of the present is most fully in play as an occasion for melancholy regret and the hope of reattunement to a form of life gone by. *Into the Forest* travels about as far with this thought as a work of fiction can go. On the other side of it, there is only trying it out for yourself.[87]

---

86. Rousseau (1979) 89.

87. I share the view of Curtis (2010) 5 that there is always an element of didaxis and the "how-to manual" in postapocalyptic fiction, which sometimes approaches the level of active encouragement to embrace the ways of the text. I also share her sense of the importance of Rousseau, and especially *The Discourse on Inequality*, for the genre as a whole, even when its influence is present in an unacknowledged form. Her reading of the ending of *Into the Forest* as apolitical infantile regression is

Among those who have tried it for themselves, much of what Theodore Kaczynski has to say on this topic is deliberately unoriginal. He is unabashed about acknowledging commonalities of thought with Jacques Ellul, for example, and claims only to have given difficult and unpalatable ideas a clearer and more accessible articulation than they would otherwise have received. But Kaczynski does believe that the practical knowledge he gained from his experience of nonpolis life allows him to make a cogent contribution to the critique of technological civilization at the level of daily life. Knowing how much time it takes to collect firewood, to prepare roots, or to tan skins allows him to formulate a more accurate account of the speculative Neolithic than green anarchists who champion Marshall Sahlins's idea of Stone Age affluence without understanding that preparation time has to be added to time spent hunting and gathering, or that in premodern societies much of this painful and laborious survival work was done by women.

When he is less occupied with critique, Kaczynski's reflections on his life in Montana are of a piece with Rousseau's rediscovery of pleasure in the sentiment of existence:

> In my life in the woods I found certain satisfactions that I had expected, such as personal freedom, independence, a certain element of adventure, and a low-stress way of life. I also achieved certain satisfactions that I hadn't fully understood or anticipated, or that even came as a complete surprise to me. The more intimate you become with nature, the more you appreciate its beauty. It's a beauty that consists not only in sights and sounds but in an appreciation of . . . the whole thing. I don't know how to express it. What is significant is that when you live

---

unfortunate, however, and neglects the careful meditation on the history and form of life of California's indigenous people that makes life in the forest first conceivable, and then practicable, for Nell and Eva. To claim that this life is "as potentially humanity ending as having everyone simply take their suicide pills as in *On the Beach*" is to misunderstand both novels in equal measure (115).

in the woods, rather than just visiting them, the beauty becomes part of your life rather than something you just look at from the outside. . . .

In living close to nature, one discovers that happiness does not consist in maximizing pleasure. It consists in tranquility. Once you have enjoyed tranquility long enough, you acquire actually an aversion to the thought of any very strong pleasure—excessive pleasure would disrupt your tranquility. . . .

Boredom is almost nonexistent once you you've become adapted to life in the woods. If you don't have any work that needs to be done, you can sit for hours at a time just doing nothing, just listening to the birds or the wind or the silence, watching the shadows move as the sun travels, or simply looking at familiar objects. And you don't get bored. You're just at peace.[88]

Kaczynski's attempt to live the life of the speculative Neolithic failed for a number of reasons, some personal, some having to do with his inability to escape the consequences of local land ownership. He saw his desire to escape from civilization as continuous with settler-colonial flight to indigenous communities, such as the one John Tanner records in his autobiography, *The Falcon*, and Crèvecoeur's reflections on indigenous sociality that Stewart offers as the epigraph to *Earth Abides*. Such desires originate in a common understanding that human beings are capable of more than they are permitted in the civilization of the polis, and that these abrogated capabilities are the source both of their discontentment with their present state and of their hope that they may relieve their posterity of even greater discontents.

The postapocalyptic sisters of *Into the Forest* encounter their indigenous predecessors on a path that leads from improvidence to surrender, and from there to the affects of dependency and

---

88. Kaczynski (2010), 405–406. On green anarchism, colonial-era white flight to indigenous communities, and taking back the "serious, practical, purposeful, life-and-death aspects of life," see 130, 289–90, 385.

contentment. Carolyn See's *Golden Days* retraces this path as dire postapocalyptic comedy. The survivors of a nuclear attack who eventually emerge from their hiding place in Topanga Canyon to the vitrified beaches of Malibu reflect:

> If any of us in this canyon knew anything, we knew that the Indians who lived here had been the last word in incompetence. No farming, no tools, no written language, no "kinship system," nothing except waterproof baskets, and that was only because they hadn't got as far as pottery. And all of us had grown up with the story of the California Indians, those dipshit Chumash who had rowed over to Catalina Island to gather shells and left a woman over there absentmindedly and didn't get back to pick her up for over twenty years.[89]

It is possible that what See's protagonist has in mind here is a garbled or misremembered version of the story of Juana Maria, the Lone Woman of San Nicolas Island, whose story is recalled in *Into the Forest*. These are, after all, the postapocalyptic memories of a narrator who was unreliable even at the best of times, and the apocalyptic event brings back to mind dim, submerged recollections of her childhood instruction in the ways of California's indigenous people. So, too, when she and her survival group find a starving feral canid that may be a dog or a coyote, they christen her Isha, because "we thought of Ishi, that last California Indian, killed with kindness by the university people up north." These recovered memories are consonant with their eventual acceptance that the apocalyptic event is a beginning, not an end—a "good time," rather than a "bad time"—because of the new forms of mentation that their occupations bring: "We'd walk without talking. I can't speak for the others, but I never thought much. When I did, it seemed the thought was absolutely new."[90]

---

89. See (1996) 182.
90. See (1996) 158, 173, 193.

While survivalists battle over who will own the ravaged agricultural lands to the east, new forms of sociality emerge along the coast, and these possibilities emerge much as they do in *Into the Forest*, as the recovery of what was already vaguely known once upon a time but consigned to the back burner—a forgotten history of California Indians, wedged between *Madame Bovary* and a book about the Spanish Civil War, or childhood memories of no use to grown-ups. There is an inexplicit analogy between the recovery of individual memory and the return to prior forms of life. Ontogeny may recapitulate phylogeny in reverse, but only partially, and opaquely to the subject of regression.

Ursula Le Guin's *Always Coming Home* has a special place in California postapocalyptic fiction that stages the return of indigenous forms of life, and the recent publication of the author's expanded edition makes the full scope of the project's ambition visible. *Always Coming Home* is a large-scale fiction—some six hundred pages in the Library of America edition, not including the additional material and supplementary essays—but it retains and exaggerates many of the generative features of Hesiod's and Mary Shelley's weak text. The expansive feeling of a world opening before you is achieved through unremitting stylistic fragmentation. The novel consists of a seemingly endless proliferation of kinds of texts: first-person emic narratives, and poems, plays, and other textual fragments that emulate salvage anthropology, are interspersed with maps, glossaries, alphabets, notes on Kesh syntax and kinship descriptions, and other such paratextual information, all of which are interrupted from time to time and conceptually reframed by the metapragmatic reflections of Le Guin's Hesiodic anthropological investigator Pandora, as she breaks cover to reflect on the goals and commitments of her project.[91]

Always Coming Home carefully revisits many of the standard tropes of postapocalyptic fiction: it reclaims the road as a place of

---

91. See Le Guin (2019) 177–78, where Pandora describes herself as married to Prometheus's brother, whom she calls Hindsight.

self-discovery; it imagines its postapocalyptic people having rediscovered the archaic catastrophism that comes from living in "a land that answers greed with drought and death"; its world is situated alongside the scars of previous misuse, with chemically poisoned no-go zones, feral dogs, and a flooded inland sea, at the bottom of which the buildings of ancient times can still be seen. Its form of the glissade is a distinctive homeostatic balance between autonomous but still accessible information machines and human populations that have their own local, discretely evolved clusters of belief.[92]

With its detailed descriptions of languages and craft skills, *Always Coming Home* is much less reticent about putting the future on show than *Earth Abides*, *Into the Forest*, or *Golden Days*. There is no one last survivor with the life experience of several epochs, but a set of peoples who are already living their own distinctive and fully exfoliated cultural futures. The reader is not left at the threshold of a life to come but plunged into the midst of it. Its inhabitants no longer know how to answer the questions Pandora addresses to them as an anthropologist of the future, but the reader understands why she is asking them. The always coming home of *Always Coming Home* is the reclamation of a California that is both the precolonial land of California's indigenous peoples, and a future in which their colonizers have accepted the environmental constraints of its landscape. This is not a land whose story is now over. Its inhabitants are still living a history that changes and develops according to the desires of the novel's diegetic agents, whether these are individuals like Stone Telling or entire peoples like the Kesh and the Condor. Not a fantasy of timeless adaptation to a landscape, in other words, but a process of continually coming home to it that is never at an end because different forms and degrees of accommodation are imagined and enacted according to the different logics in each agent's mode of self-realization.

92. Le Guin (2019) 22, 78, 166–71, 202–207, 493.

Immersing the reader directly in the future spares her the experience of the apocalypse on trial. The form of life in the valley of the Kesh is dependent on a huge reduction in the human population as compared to the present, but all that remains of these human costs are some sites of irremediable pollution and the degenerative illnesses "sevai" and "vedet." These continue to afflict the human population of the novel, but the reader does not have to live through a catastrophic die-off as a condition of arriving in the future it stages.[93] Le Guin refashions the contract between postapocalyptic writer and reader as a promise of mutual companionship:

> When I take you to the Valley, you'll see the blue hills on the left and the blue hills on the right, the rainbow and the vineyards under the rainbow late in the rainy season, and maybe you'll say, "There it is, that's it!" ... And all I will be able to say is, "Drink this water of the spring, rest here awhile, we have a long way yet to go, and I can't go without you."[94]

There is an act of faith here, that showing the future is enough, an instance of the silence at the heart of the book that Le Guin describes in her lecture "Legends for a New Land," as she reflects on the indigenous people who once inhabited the site of her family's Napa Valley ranch:

> The people who lived in the Valley are silent, now and forever. We did not listen to them. We—my people—killed them without hearing one word they said.... So at the very root and center of my book there is that: a silence, and an act of contrition. Not of reparation. There is no reparation. But inside my dance of celebration of humanity set in the dreamtime future there is another dance, a spiral going the other way into the past, not touching; a dance for the dead, in silence.[95]

---

93. Le Guin (2019) 447–48, 555–56.
94. Le Guin (2019) 398.
95. Le Guin (2019) 755–56.

The final Kesh poem in *Always Coming Home* turns toward this center of silence. The people of the dreamtime future look back to "the other people who were on earth before them," and they tell them "we were among you, coming closer, coming closer to the world." The Kesh see their own world as a flowering of historical potential unrealized in the past, and from their perspective, the past—our present—is justified as what led to themselves, a world that learned from the past, opted not to move forward, then forgot that this was ever a decision: a perfect Rousseauian outcome of what Pandora's native informant calls her "pacifist jeanjacquerie."[96]

Ontological transformation is the final promise of postapocalyptic fiction's recovery of lost capabilities. At the end of the glissade, and the precarious readaption to a historical form of life, is the hope of living differently on the earth, the joyful participation in shared life with living beings as a whole that Rousseau calls the feeling of existence. This is not a possibility that all postapocalyptic fiction embraces. In Jim Crace's *The Pesthouse* (2007), the "Dreaming Highway" along which its postapocalyptic travelers journey captures the doubleness of the road as the most evocative relic of the departed civilization—a site both of fantasy for what has been and of deadly exposure to what is. His protagonists soon learn they are better off away from "the lawless highway and the debris fields" traveled by emigrants with their barrows and wagons, and the rustlers and pirates who prey on them. They retrace their steps from the coast to the hinterland, keeping off the road as best they can on their homeward journey.[97]

Marcel Theroux's *Far North* (2009) likewise features columns on the move, masters and slaves, and women in chains. The first rule of survival is to shun the road, which will "bring you no end of trouble." In this world, the starving willingly enslave themselves, and it is the indigenous knowledge of the Tungus that offers the

---

96. Le Guin (2019) 372.
97. Crace (2007) 95–98, 229, 66, 79–87, 104–105.

best hopes for survival beyond the reach of the labor camps and of scavenging for technological remains in the polluted city of The Zone, Theroux's reimagining of the haunted site of alien landing in the Strugatsky Brothers' *Roadside Picnic* and Andrei Tarkovsky's *Stalker*. Theroux's protagonist, Makepeace, survives because she is a "savage." She has learned indigenous hunting skills, and these allow her to make her way home through the backcountry after her capture and escape, without having to expose herself to the dangers of the road.[98]

But it is Cormac McCarthy's *The Road* that most spectacularly illuminates the ways in which postapocalyptic fiction is an inheritor of the ancient motif of the road as a site of exposure. The father and son who are the protagonists of the novel make their way through a landscape ruined by the apocalyptic event, which McCarthy does not explicate except in its consequences: food production has ceased, and to survive the man and boy must discover whatever stored food has not already been looted by previous travelers. They inhabit the final phase of the glissade, reduced to the life of scavengers, without any prospect that humankind will ever again attain the level of Neolithic hunter-gatherers or primitive agrarianism. There are no more animals other than dogs scavenging like themselves, and the earth appears to be incapable of supporting the growth of plants.

In this world, postapocalyptic occupations are limited to the bare minimum of survival skills that enable forward progress. Large sections of the narrative are devoted to the upkeep of the various shopping carts the protagonists use to transport the canned goods and tarps on which they depend. The horizon of capabilities contracts to repairing a broken wheel, mending shoes, or building a concealed fire.[99] The father's insistence that he and the boy are "carrying the fire" is another echo of Hesiod. The fire

---

98. Theroux (2009) 34–36, 75, 185, 219; 232.

99. McCarthy (2006) 14–17 is one of several such sequences in which transportation devices and footwear have to be repaired or replaced. This is the "genius for fact"

is a noumenal marker of human aspiration, but only because the idea of humanity at which it gestures depends on human beings' use of literal fire. In Hesiod's poems, Prometheus steals fire from the gods and brings it to humanity hidden inside a plant stalk, after which they have to look after it for themselves.[100] Prometheus's gift is part blessing and part curse. Fire has its uses, of course, but it also implicates humankind in the constant care to maintain the level of civilization it has achieved that the man is endlessly enjoining upon the boy in McCarthy's novel. We are accustomed to the idea of modernity as Promethean (forward-thinking), not least because of Mary Shelley's *Frankenstein; or, The Modern Prometheus*, but in Hesiod's story Prometheus has a brother, Epimetheus, whose name means backward-thinking (Le Guin's Hindsight), and who is always forgetting what he is supposed to be doing. When the boy in *The Road* forgets their gun on the beach or otherwise loses track of his responsibilities, he is performing Epimethean modernity, perhaps even on purpose at times, given his occasional dubiousness about the man's Promethean intentions.

Postapocalyptic fiction is typically committed to a fairly straightforward kind of realism in order to make its point about the relationship between occupation and mentation. New forms of mentation have to be shown to emerge from new kinds of occupation. Paul Auster's *In the Country of Last Things* (1987), for example, teaches the reader how to survive in a ruined city of the Global North by stuffing your clothes with newspaper in order to stay warm, or by using a repurposed shopping cart to transport scavenged goods without it getting broken or stolen. But it also demonstrates how one person might learn these skills from another through a kind of osmosis, "in the same way as you learn a new language."[101] Didactic realism creates a particular kind of

---

that Woolf (1932) 57 points to in *Robinson Crusoe*, by which "Defoe achieves effects that are beyond any but the great masters of descriptive prose."

100. *Theogony* 507–616, *Works and Days* 42–105.
101. Auster (1987) 23, 32–33, 56–61.

dramatic tension in postapocalyptic fiction, as the teacher strives to educate the student quickly enough for this survival know-how to be useful.

In Auster's novel, this pedagogical drama is at one remove from the action. His narrator has learned survival skills on the streets, but what she is trying to communicate in her narration are meta-reflections on postapocalyptic life. These are addressed to an absent friend who is available only in writing: "Do you see what I am trying to say? In order to live you must make yourself die."[102] She inhabits a space of understanding on the far side of the horizon in which mentation is remade by occupation. The tone is appropriately urgent, but she exhorts from a position of material and cognitive security, and we do not see her mind as it is being remade by her postapocalyptic occupations.

In *The Road*, this drama unfolds in real time. The father is eminently capable, and he knows how to keep himself and the boy alive. But we feel his son slipping away from him as his mind is remade by their life on the road. The boy was born on the night of the apocalyptic event and has no knowledge of the world that preceded it. He does not understand the basic technology of a dam, or a can of Coke, while his father, we realize, is turning into the figure of the last survivor: "Maybe he understood for the first time that to the boy he was himself an alien. A being from a planet that no longer existed." Tales from this world are suspect, and the boy questions the principles on which their journey is founded. If he and his father are "the good guys," who are "carrying the fire," how come they don't help anyone they meet? To which the father can only respond by doubling down on his Gnostic ontology: "My job is to take care of you. I was appointed to do that by God. I will kill anyone who touches you."[103] They are a different kind of being from the cannibals and "roadagents" who threaten their survival.

102. Auster (1987) 20.
103. McCarthy (2006) 19–23, 153–54, 77.

The Road inhabits a gray area between historical and ontological modes of postapocalyptic fiction. The father's survivalism requires constant ontological screening of the remnants of humankind they encounter, and this brings the novel into close proximity with the survivalist fictions I examine in chapter 3. But it also invokes the anthropological and historical record through sidelong reflections on the way in which these remnants recapitulate prior forms of human life. On its opening page, father and son are "pilgrims," like the naïve westward migrants of *Blood Meridian*, and they encounter other "pilgrims" on the road. And when, in the once fertile landscape of the South, they discover partially dismembered human beings locked in a cellar for storage, the father reflects that "chattel slaves had once trod these boards bearing food and drink on silver trays." So, too, in the novel's most explicitly Hesiodic moment, what we encounter is not simply postapocalyptic horror, but postapocalyptic horror as the revealed truth of Deep History:

> Behind them came wagons drawn by slaves in harness and piled with goods of war and after that the women, perhaps a dozen in number, some of them pregnant, and lastly a supplementary consort of catamites ill clothed against the cold and fitted in dog collars and yoked each to each.[104]

Alimentation, transportation, and sexual economy reemerge as a single set of concerns, as they appear in ancient biopolitics. Hesiod recommends a slave without offspring, since one who has "calved" eats more and can't work as hard in the fields.[105] How to transport your goods on the road is of a piece with how to manage the need for copulation and expendable labor. *The Road* has deep thematic roots in antiquity, but it is language itself that does the work of historical memory here, without the need for detailed reconstruction of the historical form of life it invokes. "Catamites"

---

104. McCarthy (2006) 3, 21, 153, 168, 181, 200, 106, 91–92.
105. *Works and Days* 600–603.

suggests regression to some kind of ancient Mediterranean model, with a strict division of labor between breeding-age females reserved for reproduction and younger males employed for sexual pleasure. But nothing is explained, beyond the resonant archaism itself. Whether "man untraditional held blindly to the wrongs he had forgotten," as is the case in *Theodore Savage*, or whether the ethical glissade is something more deliberate in McCarthy's novel, we cannot know.

The deepest root that *The Road* sends into antiquity—its taproot, one might say—is the figure of the road itself. The "thousand roads of sudden death" are a postapocalyptic motif in the literature of Greco-Roman antiquity, in contrast to the Saturnian security of cave-dwelling hunter-gatherers, who are not exposed to chance encounters with human predators.[106] The urgent drama of fatherly love and filial advice in *The Road* plays out not just outside civilization, but beyond any form of sociality other than their postnuclear family unit. The survival group is a dyad, and its security, in the father's eyes, depends on maintaining its integrity. Tarps spread over their shopping cart stand in for the ancient cave.

For the greater part of *The Road*, authorial vision and the father's voice converge, but with the father's death there is a parting of the ways. A posthuman voice occupies the final pages of the novel, and it speaks of human inhabitation of the earth from a perspective other than that of human beings themselves, its latter-day pilgrims: "Once there were brook trout in the streams in the mountains.... In the deep glens where they lived all things were older than man and they hummed of mystery." The "maps and mazes" on the fishes' backs are emblems of a world that is gone—"a thing which could not be put back"—and the future that lies beyond it cannot be imagined according to forms of life in the past. *The Road* deposits the reader at the threshold of a life to come, and its puzzles are not to be explicated according to the regular modes of postapocalyptic fiction. With the death of the father, the

106. Lovejoy and Boas (1935) 58–72.

son must choose between dying alongside him and taking his chances with another group of survivors. He is still too young to engage with his father's ontology, which he can remember after his death but no longer question or challenge. We do not learn whether his father's ontological commitments are an adaptive strategy or not.[107]

Margaret Atwood's *MaddAddam* trilogy (2004–2014) is similarly reticent. Jimmy, the protagonist of *Oryx and Crake*, is a familiar kind of survivor—the last of the Americans, or perhaps even the last *Homo sapiens*, stranded in the future like Crusoe on his island. But this future belongs to the Crakers, the transgenic posthumans who are the last act of the technological civilization that perishes through the industrial sabotage perpetuated by their creator. Jimmy offers the Crakers a mythology that includes their own creation, but they understand it in ways he cannot anticipate or control. Because a whole gamut of emotional possibilities has been engineered out of their genetic makeup, they do not fill in the motivations for their own story as a pre-posthuman would. For the same reason, their social organization does not replicate structures of dominance and subordination from the past, despite Jimmy's fears that this history is destined to repeat itself. The fundamental determinant of pre-posthuman behavior, "the curious monkey brain," has been replaced with other kinds of mentation.[108]

In this world, predicting forms of life in the future based on forms of life in the past is an idle occupation for sophomoric college students, for whom it was "game over once agriculture was invented, six or seven thousand years ago." The gentle, nonjealous, uncompetitive Crakers may look like they originate in a college student's hunter-gatherer fantasy—the pre-posthuman survivors of *MaddAddam* envisage them as "indigenous people," with *Homo sapiens* as "greedy, rapacious Conquistadors." And, in a literal

---

107. McCarthy (2006) 287.
108. Atwood (2004) 106, 41, 155, 222.

sense, they do, having been meticulously engineered to retain only those features of humankind their youthful creator considered desirable. But as it turns out, this fantasy belongs to the trilogy's backstory rather than its fictional reality. Crake, their creator, perishes in the apocalyptic event, and the Crakers are not constrained by the vision of historical potential they were meant to fulfill. They have hybrid babies with the pre-posthuman survivors, and as *MaddAddam* comes to an end, they seem to be moving toward a subsistence form of life that mingles hunting and gathering with small-scale agrarianism. They have escaped their creator's intentions, and their story lies outside the narrative proper, in a world whose forms of life no one inside the novel or outside it is able to predict.[109]

MaddAddam ends with a scene of martial law. The survivalists who threaten the emergent community of pre- and posthumans are put to death at the second time of trying, but the appearance of the death penalty is not fraught with the fear of historical determinism that surrounds it in *Alas, Babylon* and *Earth Abides*, not least because the community whose will it enacts is a transgenic alliance that include the Pigoons—human/pig hybrids who have haunted the background of the trilogy as life-threatening predators but are now acknowledged as a nonhuman *ethnos* that can negotiate its own agreements with the human survivor group. The novel ends with the establishment of political alliances beyond the human, and nothing that belongs to human history alone is likely to be normative for transspecies community in the world to come. The transgenic survivors have entered a new ontic reality, which demands new forms of ontological negotiation and political commitment. They embrace new social bonds that they could not have anticipated prior to their encounter with one another. Their culturecraft is a free-adaptive response, the play of postapocalyptic fiction-making, not anxious survivalist-prepping.

109. Atwood (2014) 242, 140, 380.

3

Survivalist Anthropology

SURVIVALISM IN SPECULATIVE fiction has an even worse reputation than survivalism in real life: "Sadistic, sexist, racist, pornographic, gloating and void, survivalist fiction is an obscene parody of genuine survivalism, and a nightmare at the bottom of the barrel of sf."[1] This negative assessment has been internalized in postapocalyptic fiction. In David Brin's *The Postman*, the "armed and armored hermits" whose hobby was "thinking about the fall of society and fantasizing about what they would do after it happened," perish en masse at the hands of better-armed, better-organized groups of raiders.[2] Likewise, in Margaret Atwood's *Oryx and Crake*, Jimmy imagines the threat to the Crakers and their form of life from "survivalists who'd tuned in early, shot all comers, sealed themselves into their underground bunkers." Survivalists are "hillbillies; recluses; wandering lunatics, swathed in protective hallucinations." They are fixated on the past and in denial about the future: "Bands of nomads, following the ancient ways."[3]

But while survivalists often instantiate the threat that the past poses to the future, it is also true that survivalist fiction only "exaggerates to extremes" certain tendencies of postapocalyptic fiction

---

1. Clute and Nicholls (1999) 1118, cited in James (2000) 53.
2. Brin (1985) 44, 276.
3. Atwood (2004) 222.

more generally.[4] Its protagonists must by definition have survived the apocalyptic event, and the relationship between occupation and mentation fundamental to such fiction emerges through their efforts to keep themselves alive in the world that follows. Where these efforts fall along the axis of adversarial and communitarian human relations varies from writer to writer: Hesiod and McCarthy are at one end of the spectrum, Brin and Atwood at the other.

In this chapter, I focus on a particular kind of postapocalyptic fiction, in which the interest in survival capabilities common to such fiction as a whole is combined with an emphasis on ontological speculation on the part of its protagonists. Such fiction brackets the immediate relationship between occupation and mentation. Instead, the first task of the survivalist is an ontology that can cope with the demands of a world in which not everything that seems to be alive is really so. Survivalists must work to distance themselves from the natural human tendency to empathize with other lifeforms. They must ready themselves to encounter them as adversaries, as beings fundamentally unlike themselves, in which the appearance of a life akin to their own is a life-threatening illusion.

Vampire and zombie fictions contain the most obvious versions of the survivalist commitment to ontology. In Richard Matheson's *I Am Legend* and Colson Whitehead's *Zone One*, the survivalist's humanlike adversaries are actually nonhumans, and his senses need to be schooled if he is to keep them from entering his inner space, as if they were the lost familiars of humankind. As George Slusser has observed, however, Thoreau's *Walden* offered a fundamental model for such fictions: "In *Walden*'s survivalist experiment, Thoreau ... creates a refuge where the American individual, in order to abide, must perpetually act the role of stranger in his own land." Survivalism is not an anomaly of modern libertarian thinking in the United States but a "deep-seated cultural response to the persistent apocalyptic imagination that appears to have

---

4. James (2000) 53.

haunted even the peaceful 'experiment' of Walden Pond." *Walden* was a "training manual for the urban nightmares and armageddons of the next century," and part of its training was ontological: practical exercises in separating oneself from what appears to be alive, but in reality is not, or at least not in the same way that the survivalist is alive.[5]

Richard G. Mitchell has observed that the work of real-life survivalists is not at the level of the artifact but of culture itself. What Mitchell calls "culturecraft" has the same expansive scope as Greek epic or the mythological imagination. Its versions of community-building are comprehensive ontological projects, embracing the whole of what might, or might not, count as life and be worthy of consideration as such.[6] Fictional survivalists likewise wish to intervene in the DNA of culture, and the practice of ontology, for inclusive or exclusive purposes, is part of such work. It is from this perspective that it makes sense to consider Octavia Butler's *Parable* novels as survivalist fiction. The Earthseed writings of her protagonist, Lauren Oya Olamina, are not just an alternative theology. They reimagine survivalist ontology as a communitarian, rather than a solitary, practice. Earthseed has to be shared or it will corrupt its user, and it functions as a countercontagion in the postapocalyptic world of the novel, bringing people together where they might otherwise stand apart in hostility, while at the same time maintaining the regular claim of such fiction that survivalism always involves ontological practice.

Such considerations call for reflection on the place of cultural inheritance in individual survival. Sidner Larson has argued that American Indians are a "postapocalypse people," insofar as every single Native person has already had to articulate this relationship for themselves. The task is coeval with the emergence of

---

5. Slusser (2000) 119 and 132–34, where he compares *Walden* with the work of Richard Matheson.

6. Mitchell (2002) 9–14, 113, 213–15.

indigenous literature in North America as a kind of postapocalyptic fiction.[7] I therefore begin this chapter with an account of what communitarian autarky looks like in D'Arcy McNickle's novel of reservation life, *The Surrounded*. Seeing how survival capabilities are related to social cohesion in this novel is helpful in understanding both the way in which communitarian perspectives are suspended in survivalist fictions that take *Walden* as their model, and how they are restored in Butler's *Parable* novels.

The relationship between occupation and mentation in postapocalyptic Indian life is staged with great sensitivity in *The Surrounded*. McNickle's novel investigates the psychic consequences of the transition to reservation life on the Salish (Flathead) Reservation in western Montana. Archilde Leon returns to the reservation from Portland where he has been working as a musician to stay with his Spanish father and Indian mother. Archilde accompanies his mother on a late fall hunting trip to the mountains, where they are joined by Archilde's brother. A game warden shows up at their camp and questions their right to hunt, and in the ensuing standoff, the game warden kills Archilde's brother, and Archilde's mother kills the game warden. The killings remain undiscovered during the winter months, and in this time Archilde becomes reconciled to the traditionalism of the elders of his tribe. In spring, however, the local sheriff takes the search for the game warden's body in hand, and Archilde, his girlfriend Elise, and two of his nephews take off for the mountains, where they are quickly discovered. Elise kills the sheriff, but she and Archilde are captured by the reservation agent and an Indian policeman, who have accompanied the sheriff as backup. The nephews ride off, deeper into the mountains.

What coming to terms with reservation life means for Archilde is finding a way forward from fixation on a past life that was meaningful because it had the satisfaction of natural needs continually in view, toward the effort to preserve a living memory of this life

---

7. Larson (2000) 104, 145–46.

as something other than a culturalist simulation that Gerald Vizenor calls survivance.[8] When Archilde sets off on his hunting trip with his mother, he has a fleeting sense of the identity of their present actions with the historical life of his people. His own moving through the landscape seems to merge with the living presence of the past: "This was how it would have seemed years ago, crossing the mountains to hunt buffalo. Nothing would have been much different." But as he reflects on why he and his mother are going to hunt, his sense of continuous historical life fades and he is left with a feeling of lifeless repetition instead:

> But it was different. The mountains were empty of life, that was the difference. This ride with his mother was no more than a pleasure trip; that was the difference. If they returned without fresh meat, no one would worry; at home there were canned peas, potatoes in the cellar, and meat could be had at the butcher's; that was the difference.[9]

The historical life of the Salish seems more real than their present life. Every action in it could immediately be grasped as worth doing because it was grounded in the close presence of life and death for the tribe as a whole, in their shared life with one another, with other tribes, and with the plants and animals on which their survival depended. As his uncle Modeste sums it up for Archilde, in the present "you will die easily, but if you had lived then you might have died fighting to live." It makes no difference now whether they hunt or don't hunt. However much game they encounter, the mountains are "empty of life." Hunting is recreation without re-creation. There is no point in shooting a deer just because you can.

Archilde's disillusion originates in his inability to feel in the present the satisfaction that should come from using his capabilities in the occupations of survival. He does not fully understand its

---

8. See the discussion of Vizenor (1994) in chapter 2.
9. McNickle (2003) 116.

causes, and, as a result, he also cannot understand the commitment on the part of the old people of his tribe to perpetuating the memory of their historical form of life. He views it as a derealization of the present for the sake of a simulation of the past that has passed them by. He is unable to grasp his own melancholy and abjects it onto them. He thinks the past has usurped their present, so as to foreclose their being present to themselves, but his understanding changes when Modeste tells a story that allows him to see the lived reality of this life for himself:

> For the first time he had really seen it happen. First the great numbers and the power, then the falling away, the battles and the starvation in the snow, the new hopes and the slow facing of disappointment, and then no hope at all, just this living in the past. He had heard the story many times, but he had not listened. It had tired him. Now he saw that it had happened and it left him feeling weak. It destroyed his stiffness toward the old people. He sat and thought about it and the flames shot upward and made light on the circle of black pines.[10]

Archilde understands care for a historical form of life as survivance. Survivance makes it possible for him to recover a shared life in the present that is grounded in this care. He looks after his relatives when they come to his house after his mother's death, and he looks out for his young nephews during their flight to the mountains. With the discovery of survivance as care, Archilde also discovers that "he too belonged to the story of *Sniél-emen*," the mountains of the surrounded, as they are called in the novel's epigraph. But Archilde belongs to *Sniél-emen* tragically. His retreat with Elise and his nephews into a "high, snug canyon" in the mountains—the valley of the Salish in miniature—is cut short by the appearance of Quigley the sheriff, and, in his train, the reservation agent and the Indian policeman. The apprehension of a pre-Christian, prereservation shared life that guided him to the mountains will

10. McNickle (2003) 74.

not perdure without a grounding in material existence that he cannot provide, and he is forced to acknowledge a truth that his nephews had seen more clearly than he had in the eyes of the priest who taught them "how much greater—how everlasting—was the world of priests and schools, the world which engulfed them."[11]

For the surrounded, there is no place to hide, but Archilde does not misunderstand survivance as a commitment to reenacting a historical form of life when it is impossible to do so in the present. His fate is tragic because he is haunted by an action that precedes his understanding of survivance as care, and which cuts short his ability to perpetuate it nontragically. In the end, he sees through the culture trap and understands that what his uncle has staged for him as a story is a form of life—a way of living and acting and using the body, not a set of beliefs that as a modern person he cannot participate in.

At the outset of *The Surrounded*, Archilde identifies his tribe's relictualized form of life with the small herd of buffalo that is colocated with them on the reservation, behind the wire enclosure of a biological survey. His uncle and his mother "were not real people," just as "buffaloes were not real to him either," since they too are now cordoned off in a reserve instead of moving freely through their world. The buffaloes "had been real things to his mother, and to the old people," but they, like the old people themselves, have been absorbed into the fantasmatic life of the past. Later, when Archilde withdraws temporarily into the badlands on the edge of the reservation to reflect on his experiences since his return, he finds a half-starved mare with her foal and attempts to rescue her against her will. He ropes her and leads her back to his camp, where she dies:

> In the end he wore her down. And when finally she stopped, with quivering legs braced and her eyes glaring, the anger and will to overcome which the chase had aroused in him collapsed.

---

11. McNickle (2003) 275, 286.

He was left limp and ashamed.... She groaned aloud, a final note of reproach for the ears of the man who had taken it upon himself to improve her condition.[12]

The action does not succeed in its goal, but as a relationship of action, Archilde's engagement with the horse allows an understanding of his own situation in relation to his people to emerge, whereas he could not cathect to the derealized, hyperreal buffalo that he could only access through speculation. A version of this scene recurs in James Welch's *Winter in the Blood*. The novella is set on the Fort Belknap reservation in northern Montana, and its unnamed protagonist's efforts to feel at home there culminate in an apprehension of shared life with his horse in the common harm that has been done to both of them alike:

> A cow horse. You weren't born that way; you were born to eat your grass and drink slough water, to nip the other horses in the flanks the way you do the lagging bulls, to mount the mares. So they cut off your balls to make you less temperamental, though I think they failed at that. They haltered you, blindfolded you, waved gunnysacks at you and slapped you across the neck, the back with leather. Finally they saddled you—didn't you try to kick them when they reached under your belly for the cinch?—and a man climbed on you for the first time. Only you can tell me how it felt to stand quivering under the weight of that first man, dumbfounded until—was it?—panic and anger began to spread through your muscles and you erupted, rearing, lunging, sunfishing around the corral until the man had dug a furrow with his nose in the soft, flaky manure. You must have felt cocky, proud, but the man—who was it?—surely not First Raise—the man climbed on your back again and began to rake you with his spurs. Again you reared and threw the man; again he dusted himself off and climbed back on. Again and again, until you were only crowhopping and running and swerving and the man

12. McNickle (2003) 62, 24–42.

clung to the saddle horn and jerked your head first one way, then the other, until you were confused and half-blind with frustration. But you weren't through. There was the final step—turn him out, somebody said, you heard it—and you raced through the open gate, down the rutted road, your neck stretched out as though you were after a carrot, and the man's spurs dug deep in your ribs. You ran and ran for what must have seemed like miles, not always following the road, but always straight ahead, until you thought your heart would explode against the terrible constriction of its cage. It was this necessity, this knowledge of death, that made you slow down to a stiff-legged trot, bearing sideways, then a walk, and finally you found yourself standing under a hot sun in the middle of a field of foxtail and speargrass, wheezing desperately to suck in the heavy air of a summer's afternoon. Not even the whirr of a sage hen as it lifted from a clump of rosebush ten feet away could make you lift that young tired head.

A cow horse.[13]

There is no more magical realism in *Winter in the Blood* than there is in *A Farewell to Arms*. Yet this passage is properly understood as the voice of a horse. Not the projection of a human voice into an animal but human speech made the organ of communication for another life-form. The unobtrusiveness of the realist novella allows the reader to grasp the understanding between human being and horse revered in Plains Indian culture without making it into a lifeless, determinist cultural simulation. The protagonist's apprehension of the possibility of a single biography not just for himself and his horse, but for horses and Indians as a whole, has as its deep background the knowledge that other animals as well as human beings were once called peoples.[14] The horizon of

13. Welch (1974) 114–15.
14. *Oyáte*, "people" or "nation," is the regular term for other animal groups in Lakota, for example. As Ingold (2000) 49 observes, such terminology is unlikely to be a projection of human social ambience onto "the mirror of nature," which is then

shared life that once embraced political alliances beyond the human has shrunk to commonalities of suffering between singular beings, but part of the novella's staging of shared life in its tragic modality is its acknowledgment of just this limitation and its not shrinking away from the face with which shared life does in fact draw close in the present. This is what survivance looks like. The suggestion that tragic apprehension of shared life with living beings as a whole might open up the form of the novella to a kind of story it cannot actually accommodate is a kind of trickster poetics—it lets something happen, without explaining why it is possible.

Whereas the revivifications of hunter-gatherer life in the postapocalyptic fictions examined in chapter 2 are straight-up speculative anthropology, the animal encounters of *The Surrounded* and *Winter in the Blood* function as the internal anthropology of survivance rediscovered in opposition to the cultural simulations of ethnography. They stage the internal other of historical memory preserved by the body and made accessible through action. The recovery of shared life with living beings as a whole is consonant with the sentiment of existence in the mainstream of postapocalyptic fiction and has a manifestly ontological dimension as the reframing of human being within these larger horizons. This reframing is not explicitly articulated as an ontology—as survivance, the novels' multispecies ethnography is enacted, not mentalized—but it is an implicit ontology nonetheless; not an acquisitive conquest of new powers of mind but a restoration of forgotten attachments.

This reparative cathexis stands in contrast to the work of adversarial ontology in survivalist fiction. Identifying a model for such fiction in *Walden*, George Slusser locates a starting point for

---

somehow forgotten or disavowed as a projection, but is rather an acknowledgment of the ways in which other animals live in social groups like those of human beings. Aristotle's "political animals" also include nonhumans, such as bees, wasps, and cranes (*History of Animals* 488a8–9).

Thoreau's survivalist thinking in Emerson's claim that society is a conspiracy against "the manhood of every one of its members," since "no law can be sacred to me but that of my nature." For this law to prevail, Slusser argues, "the self that proclaims it has to continue to exist, even beyond the existence of that nature of which he is presumably a part: in other words, to *survive*." *Walden* is a manual for the perdurance of an absolute self beyond all claims of duties and natural needs, of living attachments and material dependence. Rather than grounding lasting forms of social cohesion, the goal of autarky here is to produce a self that can remain itself beyond any and all communitarian claims. Identifying threats to its protagonist's project of absolute selfhood is therefore at the very heart of the project of *Walden*, and such threats are eliminated through the articulation and enactment of the adversarial ontology that Slusser calls "acts of imagination."[15]

Walden endeavors to prove the claim that its author has remained faithful to the law of his nature by merging the journal with the account book. Whereas you, dear reader, have made the law of your nature submissive to others and are now "the slave-driver of yourself,"[16] *Walden* is a ledger that will pass any audit for living truly, or truly living. Adversarial accounting is a therapy for the empathy that would otherwise distract you from the work of realizing your nature. It keeps other lives at a distance by insisting that only what it records is really life.

Thoreau shies away from relationships of animal husbandry, like those of *The Surrounded* and *Winter in the Blood:* "I should never have broken a horse or bull and taken him to board for any work he might do for me, for fear I should become a horse-man or herds-man merely." Long-term commitment to others, whether as

---

15. Slusser (2000) 119–20. Hay (2017) 175–76 analyzes continuities of *Walden*'s survivalist themes with those of antebellum postapocalyptic writing and notes that Thoreau's cabin makes an appearance in the postapocalyptic role-playing game *Fallout 4*.

16. Thoreau (1991) 8.

master or partner, entails being gradually transformed by that relationship in ways that are hard to keep in sight and retain control over. By keeping yourself pure, however, as a *puer aeternus*—a Peter Pan figure free of grown-up attachments—you prepare the stage for those magical moments in which this self can both perform and witness the spectacular transfigurations that originate in itself alone. What is truly alive does not work itself patiently into something else. Instead, it undergoes sudden metamorphosis, like Walden Pond, which "was dead and is alive again," or the insect that emerges fully formed from the farmer's table, astounding the family gathered around it.[17]

The culminating vision of Nature in *Walden* is a spectacular instance of Moloch mind. Thoreau revels in the contemplation of zoological life consuming itself for the delight of an observer who stands outside its claims to participation and community:

> I love to see that Nature is so rife with life that myriads can be afforded to be sacrificed and suffered to prey on one another; that tender organizations can be so serenely squashed out of existence like pulp,—tadpoles which herons gobble up, and tortoises and toads run over in the road; and that sometimes it has rained flesh and blood.[18]

The visionary perspective of one who stands outside life is the reward for the unremitting therapy of empathy that would otherwise undo life's otherness to the observer. It is predicated upon the imaginary violence that Thoreau constantly directs toward other life-forms that cross his path as a kind of ontological exercise.[19]

---

17. Thoreau (1991) 47, 156–57, 177, 250, 267.
18. Thoreau (1991) 256.
19. The following tally is probably not complete: severed heads cauterized with hot iron and crushed (6); legs broken in a powerful press (22); the rags of a soldier hit by a cannon ball (23); a collapsing floor (32); Egyptians drowned in the Nile and their bodies fed to dogs (48); a fox that left its foot in a trap and a muskrat that gnawed its leg (54); a house as a trap into which one puts a paw (55); blood infected with the virus of helping others (61); Indians burned at the stake (61); infection with

This is the therapeutic violence of writing that he characterizes elsewhere in a remark about Goethe "striking out the heart of life at a blow, as the Indian takes off a scalp," noting that "I feel as if my life had grown more outward when I can express it."[20] Writing as therapeutic violence enacts the requisite adversarial ontology, sustaining the I that, in *Walden*, insists it is the one thing in the landscape that is truly alive, and the one thing that is therefore truly deserving of life. Other people are so far from being alive that Thoreau recommends they sleep in coffins: "I am far from jesting," he adds.[21]

Because Thoreau has more life—is more truly alive—than those around him, his own life is a visionary predation that thrives on the sacrificial offering of others. But this visionary position requires constant testing and careful maintenance. The best way to decide whether something that appears to be alive is truly living is to determine whether it is profitable. To really live requires surplus time, and so in any life you should calculate how much of it has been spent uselessly on what could have been more easily acquired "with proper management." Thoreau has "more lives to live" because he is better than other people at doing what he does all day.[22]

The original meaning of *logos* (precept) is, as Thoreau constantly reminds us, accounting, and he, like Crusoe, is a strict bookkeeper of his own existence. By being more capable than

---

Saint Vitus's dance (76); having one's eyes gouged out as a way of seeing that one has only the rudiment of an eye (77); the bullet of thought enters the ear of the hearer (114); the horizon infected with a cankerous disease (130); a Mexican spitted with relish (130); going into town as running the gauntlet (137); a lance thrust between the ribs of a bloated pest (156); a woodchuck eaten raw (170); an old wiseacre beaten with a trowel (194); the brain as fruit offered for sale (215); tortoises and toads run over in the road, and a rain of flesh and blood (256); shooting one's self (257); light that puts out our eyes (267).

20. Cited in Sayre (1977) 53.

21. Thoreau (1991) 26. Cf. "No wise man has yet learned any thing of absolute value by living.... I have lived some thirty years on this planet, and I have yet to hear the first syllable of valuable or even earnest advice from my seniors" (9).

22. Thoreau (1991) 42.

others, he produces the surplus time to do what they cannot do, so that he lives more—is more alive—than they are.[23] The *logos* of accounting and the *logos* of experience are one, as Melville saw in his double portrait of Emerson and Thoreau as master and apprentice of creative bookkeeping in *The Confidence-Man*: "If still in golden accents old Memnon murmurs his riddle, none the less does the balance-sheet of every man's ledger unriddle the profit or loss of life."[24] Thoreau's accounts are anything but "parodies of America's methods of evaluation," as Stanley Cavell suggests.[25] They are America's method of evaluation ("freedom isn't free"), and Thoreau has played his part in making them so.

If I am indubitably alive, but everyone else is much less so, contact with others may infect me with what they have. The most prudent course of action is to dodge or destroy them (if only as an imaginative exercise), until their being really alive can be tested, and the "experiment of living" verified. Being more alive than others is always agonistic and performative, and the adversarial quality of *Walden*'s double ledger no doubt accounts for the frequency with which it has been imitated. Emulation is a way of contesting its author's claim to inimitability.[26]

23. The following tally is probably not complete either: paying the least amount possible for the materials for one's home (41); doing better than "any farmer in Concord did that year" (44) and the next year "better still" (46); acquiring furniture that "cost me nothing of which I have not rendered an account" (54); knowing the price of everything because one keeps one's accounts on one's thumbnail (67), whereas the nation is ruined "by want of calculation" (75). This is the everyday vigilance toward one's neighbors that makes time to "suck out all the marrow of life" (74).

24. Melville (1990) 234.

25. Cavell (1992) 30. Cavell is hardly the only reader who is unwilling to accept Thoreau's accounts at face value. Bennett (1994) 30 takes them to prefigure "Heidegger's critique of enframing," and even Friedrich (2008), who wants to show that there are "values that are straightforwardly affirmed and rarely questioned, mocked, or parodied" in *Walden* (35), thinks they are a "parody of Ben Franklin" (50).

26. Buell (1996) 311–96 analyzes the *Walden* meme at some length, so I will not dwell on it here. It lives on anyway, in spite of its author. The blurb to Fate (2011)

Nathaniel Hawthorne investigates the relationship between the absolute self of survivalism and the adversarial ontology on which it depends in his last romance. Called *Septimius Felton* and *Septimius Norton* in its two near-complete variants, it is the story of a man "who was resolved never to die."[27] The rudiments of the story were told to him by Thoreau, as the biography of a former inhabitant of Hawthorne's house, the Wayside, and in his notes, Hawthorne considered using the device of the found manuscript to write up the story, as if he had discovered it "in the process of making repairs and additions." These notes conflate the protagonist of the story with Thoreau himself (he refers to it as "Thoreau's legend"),[28] and, in the extant versions of the romance, he shifts its location from the Wayside to the vicinity of Walden Pond, dropping the found manuscript idea for regular third-person narration, and backdating its setting to the Revolutionary War, whose ferment is a thin veil for contemporary turmoil in the onset of the Civil War.[29]

---

invites readers to "imagine Thoreau married, with a job, three kids, and a minivan . . . as the author seeks to apply the hermit-philosopher's insights to a busy modern life." Fate himself (2011) xii actually cites Thoreau's "I would not have anyone adopt my mode of living" but hopes that, were Thoreau alive today, he might be "a bit curious" about his own efforts to replicate him.

27. Hawthorne (1977) 499. Differences between the two versions are discussed in the editorial appendices to the Centenary edition. I refer to both versions, as well as Hawthorne's notes for planning, expanding, and developing them, since all three are useful in divining his ambitions for a project that never quite took final form in its author's mind.

28. Hawthorne (1977) 504. These notes (Study 2, as the editors title it) contain a character sketch of the protagonist ("a very narrow man, but of great strength of purpose"), reasons for his growing apart from the world (loss of first love), his plans for a minimalist dwelling ("a hut of boughs"), the form the discovered manuscript might take ("a journal, extending over a long series of years"), and the attachment to the locality it reveals ("He shall perhaps have strong affinities for earth, a love of the soil, of this particular spot, of the house which he himself has built on it").

29. As Gollin (2005) 172 observes, Hawthorne's notes actually refer to the Revolutionary War in the narrative as "the civil war."

The protagonist of *Septimius Felton* is engaged in a quest for the elixir of life. Septimius views the elixir not as a miracle, or a perversion of nature, but as evidence to humankind that "Nature had intended, by innumerable ways, to indicate to us the great truth that death was an alien misfortune, a prodigy, a monstrosity, into which man had only fallen by defect, and that even now, even [*sic*] if a man had a reasonable portion of his original strength in him, he might live forever, and scorn death."[30] The shortness of life prevents Septimius from becoming a person of a particular kind. He is unwilling to devote himself to one thing or another because, with a limited life span, choosing one occupation entails rejecting a host of others. The elixir will enable him to become fully human at last by obviating the need for choice. Without the prospect of death, he can be, in turn, Don Juan, billionaire, philosopher, world leader, historian, prophet, criminal, and master inventor, before finally turning to death for some new source of variety once the interest of the world has been exhausted and life appears to repeat itself.[31] Becoming an unlimited series of particular persons will not compromise his absolute selfhood.

As Septimius reflects on the war around him, he contrasts his "mystic hopes" for endless life with the "air of the battlefield" and acknowledges that to "live the full, free, generous life of humanity" has as one of its conditions "to share all the liabilities of his fellow men." What he never grasps, however, is the converse: that to choose lives instead of a life is to exist in a state of latent murderousness toward those who have made the opposite decision. His commitment to self-maximization takes him "out of the category of the rest of the human race" and fills him with the sense that the life which surrounds him is not really life at all. When an English officer flirts with a girl from his village, Septimius ambushes him

---

30. Hawthorne (1977) 15. The second "even" is extremely suspect. The editors (677) note that "of" in "a reasonable portion of his original strength" is an addition in Sophia Hawthorne's hand.

31. Hawthorne (1977) 170–76.

at gunpoint while at the same time protesting himself innocent of the desire to harm him. His claim—"I have no enmity toward you"—prompts an incredulous reply: "Then why are you here with your gun among the shrubbery?" The officer insists upon a duel, and Septimius kills him, all the while continuing to proclaim his innocence: "I had no thought of this—no malice towards you in the least."[32]

Despite appearances to the contrary, Septimius is not a hypocrite. The part of him that kills and the part of him that speaks of killing are divided from each other. He feels "a tingling in his being" that signals the impending violence and senses that what he feels is somehow at odds with his "intended profession ... of peace," but he does not, and cannot, acknowledge the violence as his own. War is "a stream rushing past him," and even if he plunged into its midst, "he would not be wet by it." His pursuit of truly living bereaves him of the ability to recognize even ordinary human aggression for what it is, let alone understand his own murderousness that is not accompanied by feelings of rage.[33]

Septimius Felton cleaves to *Walden*'s adversarial accounting. Having more life than others is what makes life worth living, and having more life than others is only possible through therapeutic violence. *Septimius Norton*, however, undermines the very idea that living more truly is possible by having more lives to live. In this version, Hawthorne develops the backstory of Septimius's

---

32. Hawthorne (1977) 130, 501, 26–27.

33. Hawthorne (1977) 17–23. Septimius's lack of involvement in the issues of the Revolutionary War has parallels with the strange blend of antislavery sentiment and anti-activism in Hawthorne's attitude to the Civil War, as Reynolds (2005) 41–44 and Gollin (2005) 170–72 observe. However, as Septimius erupts into violence in the midst of his professed quietism, he looks less like an image of his author's response to his times. Gollin (2005) 175 goes on to suggest that Hawthorne is "exploring an atavistic component in the American character" through Septimius's Indian ancestry, but this suggestion falls short of the ambitions of Hawthorne's diagnosis, since Septimius's ancestor, the first to sacrifice the life of another in order to extend his own, is a pure-blooded Englishman who has yet to depart for the colonies.

English ancestor. He discovers the recipe for the elixir and is able to manufacture it by sacrificing the life of his beloved. Afflicted thereafter with a bloody footstep that marks his passage, he flees to America in the early colonial period where he establishes himself as chief of a New England Indian tribe. Over several generations, this "great Sagamore," known as "the Undying One," is able to inculcate a state of absolute good order among his Indian subjects, despite having to continually change the "bloody moccasin" that betokens the source of his knowledge of the good.[34]

The tribe, however, whose self-appointed guardian the Sagamore has become, finds this life in which they are always wisely governed "tedious and wearisome beyond all idea," and they do their best to get rid of the "tedious old Sagamore." Since he is immortal, this is a hopeless task, and Hawthorne enjoys himself tremendously describing the Indians' efforts to shoot, beat, and burn to death their philanthropic savior. In due course, the Sagamore perceives the hopelessness of his project of promoting universal happiness through his transmitted wisdom and consents to depart. Speaking to those he is about to leave behind as if "from another state of being," he tells them they have taught him what he had not yet learned, in all his years of patient inquiry—that humankind is unable to learn in any other way than by experience. Disappointed that he has lived so long for the sake of such a "poor, dreary, little bit of wisdom as this," he quits them forever, leaving the secret of the elixir with his great-great-great-great-grandson.[35]

After the Sagamore's departure, the tribe's enemies descend upon them, followed by a plague, and then the English. They find all these misfortunes preferable to being perfected in virtue through the precepts of the Sagamore. In fact, it is only when they think they are killing him that the tribe finds something to admire in their guardian, as he appears to have finally discovered the virtue of silence. As the Sagamore sits in the flames, the tribe think

---

34. Hawthorne (1977) 358.
35. Hawthorne (1977) 356–61.

"how quietly and majestically he had died, as an Indian warrior ought, leaving his incombustible body as a memorial of the great soul that had breathed out in a whirlwind of fire." For a moment, the Sagamore's relationship to knowledge appears to be iconic, not discursive. Rather than giving them "instructions for war and for peace, for hunting and planting, and how to build their wigwams in a better fashion," he lets his body stand for the achievement of knowledge in life without the desire to burden future generations with that knowledge, which can only produce the misery of subservience to those who have come before.[36]

Hawthorne's Indians are icons of understanding, not fountains of good advice. They offer no accounts of what they know or what they are capable of. They do not make life into a contest, a competition to see who has more life and who is more truly alive. They embrace the brevity of life and the limits of mortal self-realization. As a result, other life does not become background scenery to their own visionary experiences. Septimius, by contrast, undergoes the same derealization of other life-forms that is the price of visionary predation in *Walden*, and Hawthorne figures this experience in the obsessional landscape of Thoreau's journal, the troubled surface of Walden Pond itself:

> If part of his life, and that which seemed as solid as any other, was an illusion, then why not all. It was, in short, a moment with Septimius such as many men have experienced, when something that they deemed true and permanent appearing suddenly questionable, the whole scenery of life shakes, jars, grows tremulous, almost disappears in mingled and confused colors, as when a stone is thrown into the smooth mirror of Walden Lake, and seems to put in jeopardy the surrounding hills, woods, and the sky itself. True; the scene soon settles itself again, and looks as substantial as before; but a haunting doubt is apt to keep close at hand, persecuting us forever with that

---

36. Hawthorne (1977) 360–61.

query—"Is it real! Can I be sure of it? Did I not behold it once on the point of dissolving?"[37]

At the heart of the vision of "more lives to lead" that the elixir affords is an intimation of the vision's costs: what had appeared to be alive is not really or truly so, in contrast to the visionary perspective of the observer. Life becomes "scenery," and other lives never regain their substantial kinship with his own. This loss of reality is what Hawthorne exposes as the undisclosed cost—the externality or ledger-de-main—of *Walden*'s pursuit of what is truly living.

Hawthorne imagines a materialist reduction of *Walden*'s visionary predation: ingesting the mixture of plant matter and human blood stipulated by the recipe for the elixir will automatically produce the sacrificial ontology staged in Thoreau's journal. Horror fiction, by contrast, hypostasizes his conceit of lives that are more and less alive by turning them into distinct ontic kinds. The visionary separation that adversarial ontology and therapeutic violence produce and maintain is the basic scenario of posthuman survivalist fiction, in which a lack of life in what appears to be alive indicates a different order of being entirely: the vampire or the zombie.

If survivalist fiction "exaggerates to extremes" the tendencies of postapocalyptic fiction more generally, this is largely a consequence of the distinctive *mise-en-scène* that emerges from the fusion of the occupational focus of *Robinson Crusoe* with the ontological practice of *Walden*.[38] The story of a single character who is really alive will mostly be about what this character does all day, and how they survive by keeping their distance from those who are less alive than themselves. Robert Neville, the protagonist of Richard Matheson's *I Am Legend*, iterates the details of the "tiresome and monotonous work" required to keep himself alive in the

37. Hawthorne (1977) 354.
38. James (2000) 53.

face of the vampire hordes that have taken over Los Angeles. He works through his to-do list for the day, which is much like his to-do list for the day before, and the day after, and the day after that. Work is "something to lose himself in," and by virtue of his repetitive occupations he slowly comes to feel that he is turning into a new man. He is coming to accept the present, now that he is "his own ethic," enacting the Emersonian refusal to submit to any law but that of his own nature.[39]

Neville's prepping is immaculate: he armors his house securely; he installs a freezer, a generator, an electric stove, and a water tank; he builds a hothouse and a workbench; he burns down the houses on either side of him without damage to his own; he collects records and books to entertain himself, and lays in huge stores of canned goods to survive on. But his comparison of himself to "a weird Robinson Crusoe, imprisoned on an island of night surrounded by oceans of death," suggests the danger that lies on the horizon. He is an entirely competent survivalist when it comes to the business of staying alive, but his ontological separation is incomplete and compromised by longing for someone to share his solitude with him.[40]

Neville believes at first that he has successfully navigated the transition from hunted to hunter and that the robe of the warrior hermit fits him snugly. He thinks he likes his sequestration and that he is a more or less happy bachelor vampire slayer, "afraid of the possible demand that he make sacrifices and accept responsibility again." He has learned "to stultify himself to introspection," as he thinks a good survivalist should, by focusing on the present and the tasks at hand, so that occupation may produce new forms of mentation. But the process doesn't work. His problem is not simply involuntary celibacy, but the fact that his desire for sex with vampire women takes the form of a longing to be reunited with his dead wife. He is threatened by desire when particular individuals

---

39. Matheson (1995) 16, 23, 62–64.
40. Matheson (1995) 96, 83.

among the undead resemble her and seem to offer, not just sex, but connection to the lost world of the living.[41]

What undermines Neville's security is a temptation to "be one" with the nonhuman lives that surround him, a desire that resonates with his Poundian claim to be "a man, not a destroyer," however much it may look otherwise under present circumstances. The first manifestation of this longing is the risky enterprise of luring a dog to his house, so that he can reenact the Deep History of animal domestication. Even his metaphors betray him. He imagines the outcome of his practice of ontological separation as "bovinity," or becoming "predominantly vegetable"—figures of connection to shared life with living beings as a whole, rather than separation from them. He is finally snared, blocking out the telltale signs that what he wants to believe is a human survivor is in fact a vampire woman sent by the new posthuman society to entrap him and put an end to his lethal ways.[42]

Neville suffers the ultimate indignity. Rather than reducing the posthumans to the law of his nature, he becomes an item in their ontology. The familiar postapocalyptic trope in which the present becomes mythological for the generations that succeed the original survivors is subjected to a biomaterialist reversal. For the posthuman survivors of *I Am Legend*—a new life-form that succeeds both the old human beings and the pure vampires who preyed on them—it is they themselves who are the survivalists, "repossessing society by violence," like a revolutionary vanguard. Neville will be cemented into the foundation myths of their new society in order to preserve its primitive spirit, group will, and cohesion. Because of his alien blood he becomes "a new terror born in death, a new superstition entering the unassailable fortress of forever," but it is their culturecraft that turns him into a legend.[43]

41. Matheson (1995) 117, 139.
42. Matheson (1995) 29, 140, 96, 121.
43. Matheson (1995) 166–70.

The protagonist of Colson Whitehead's *Zone One* is a self-described "survivalist even at an early age." Mark Spitz is not, however, a grizzled white longbeard from the backwoods of Oregon but a thirtysomething African American man from the suburban tristate area. The survivalism under the microscope in *Zone One* is his ability to translate the alienation and disinterest that made him an altogether typical also-ran in the world before the apocalypse into one of the success stories of life after global zombification. His genius consists in his capacity to turn his recognition that life after zombies differs from life before them only in degree, not kind, into immediate and decisive action. By constantly reminding himself of the precepts that kept him safely unattached in the earlier world, he can prosper and flourish in the more obviously survivalist scenarios that have succeeded it.[44]

At a superficial level, Mark Spitz's capabilities are straightforwardly practical. Being a hunter-gatherer in the new world is not all that different from foraging for rent money and ramen in the old one. At a deeper level, however, the key to his survival is ontological separation, and he has a long history of success in this regard. Whereas Robert Neville had to force himself to unsee his wife's face in the faces of the female vampires, Mark Spitz always found it difficult to regard his partners as truly alive:

> In the time before the flood, Mark Spitz had a habit of making his girlfriends into things that were less than human. There was always a point, sooner or later, when they crossed a line and became creatures.... They had been replaced by this familiar abomination, this thing that shared the same face, same voice, same familiar mannerisms that had once comforted him. To anyone else, the simulation was perfect. If he tried to make his case ... the world would indulge his theory, even participate in a reasonable-sounding test.... But he would know. He knew where they failed in their humanity. He would

---

44. Whitehead (2011) 9, 14.

leave.... There was no way they could convince him they were human.⁴⁵

Mark Spitz's "healthiest" relationship is postapocalyptic. They share the pursuit of common needs—for food, water, fire, and a shelter they can secure against zombies. The simplification of shared life to an existence that is continuously meaningful because it is enacted within the horizon of life and death fosters relationality. But when his companion does not return from a solo foraging expedition, he does not allow his regrets to jeopardize his survival in a world he experiences as an arena for his own capabilities. This world affords him the opportunity to act directly and decisively on his pre-apocalyptic intimation that others are less alive than he is. Therapeutic violence no longer needs to be repressed. It can now be embraced as philanthropy—making the world safe for those who are truly living.

Mark Spitz lives an exceptionally lucid version of apocalyptic time. He understands that the freedoms of postapocalyptic life are the flourishing he had always dreamed of but never been able to fully enact: "I've always been like this. Now I'm more me." He is named for a capability of which he was thought incapable in the world before the apocalypse: "The black-people-can't-swim-thing."⁴⁶ He is a swimmer in the same way Thoreau is a basket maker when he claims "I too had woven a kind of basket of a delicate nature."⁴⁷ Both are marked by the trace of agonistic confrontations with what they had not done or could not do, and translate the capabilities involved into a claim to a higher-level, metaphorical version of the skill in question. Mark Spitz quickly becomes an expert marksman, and his spectacular clearance of a clogged section of I-95 is compared to the work of his companion in arms, the Quiet Storm, a post-live art installation artist who

---

45. Whitehead (2011) 194.
46. Whitehead (2011) 197, 231. On Whitehead's reworking of race and the zombie novel, see Hoberek (2012).
47. Thoreau (1991) 18.

arranges abandoned vehicles into Nazca-like patterns only visible from the air. The emergence into full play of what was blocked, occluded, and held back in their prior life is a pure flowering of apocalyptic time. Here, among the "slow desperadoes and fellow sheriffs, meting out justice in the territory," their simple occupations are as serious, their simple objects as beautiful as they can be.[48]

Zone One hits the high notes of postapocalyptic fiction with effortless ease. But it also shows how high-modernist perspectives on modernity were always already enmeshed with sub-elite genres of popular imagination. The epigraph from Ezra Pound's "Hugh Selwyn Mauberley" that announces part 2—"The age demanded an image | of its accelerated grimace"—draws attention to high modernism as a site of apocalyptic visions, just as Robert Neville's Poundian claim to be "a man, not a destroyer" is carefully folded into the characterology of *I Am Legend*. Whitehead returns the reader to high modernism's project of exposing modernity for what it really is with a literalizing biomaterialist twist. T. S. Eliot's *The Waste Land* asks its readers: "Are you alive, or not?" Mark Spitz's commanding officer informs his subordinates that the reason the zombies walk around the city the way they do is "because they're too stupid to know they're dead."[49] Vernacularization makes the tracking of cultural decline into a game of dumb and dumberer in which the diagnostic text is itself a player.

Zone One maps the high-modernist poets' river of humanity back onto the crowded spaces of the American city. The "dark tsunami" that streams down Broadway at the end of the novel is Eliot's "crowd flowed over London Bridge," with its ontological code finally unlocked by apocalyptic time: "I had not thought death had undone so many." Modernism blooms anew, fulfilling the prophecy of its vernacular ancestors. Melville's "all-fusing spirit of the West, whose type is the Mississippi itself," was likewise "one

---

48. Whitehead (2011) 131.
49. Whitehead (2011) 217.

cosmopolitan and confident tide," in which every face "looked like the yeasty crest of a billow."[50]

The Confidence-Man is already tracking zombification, which makes a mockery of the American *comédie humaine*, revealing instead the extractive process by which the capabilities of the many are operationalized as resources of the One. If, as Lawrence Buell has argued, the "unkillable dream" of the Great American Novel has as its characteristic icon a *tableau vivant* of national diversity, then the River of Humanity is its counterimage, the return of the repressed as the undead, in all their sameness.[51] Other lives turn insubstantial and flow into one another. Whitehead gives us *Walden*'s vision—"the life in us is like the water in the river"—as a survivalist call to arms. The terminal vision of *Zone One* is a border wall about to be submerged by a river of posthumans, the settlement about to be washed away as the tides of life beyond the frontier sweep over it at last.

The survivors of *Zone One* find satisfaction in the exercise of the capabilities that keep the Others at bay. These capabilities are both physical and ontological, and they work together to create a virtuous cycle of self-preservation. This cycle can in turn lead to new forms of sociality among the survivors if they are honest with themselves, acknowledging that the plague's "recalibration of faculties" only "honed the underlying qualities" of each of them.

Emergent forms of shared life have to be rigorously policed for authenticity. Mark Spitz shelters for a while with a local survivor group but recognizes immediately that their community will not last because its leaders include "one of those apocalypse-as-moral-hygiene people" who believes "the human race deserved the Plague," and that "we brought it on ourselves for poisoning the planet, for the Death of God, the calculated brutalities of the global economic system, for driving primordial species to

50. Whitehead (2011) 245; Melville (1990) 14, 275.
51. Buell (2008) 142–43.

extinction." This belief creates a desire in him to prove that he is one of the elect who are exempt from judgment. He opens the doors to the zombies, killing everyone except Mark Spitz, who saw the disaster coming.[52]

It is crucial to Mark Spitz's survival that his ontology is his own, not someone else's ready-to-hand ideology. The ontological calculus of *Zone One* is simple. The survival of one requires an ontology of one, and all forms of collective culturecraft, from local do-goodism to the Reconstruction US government, are fake and counteradaptive to survival. The phony American phoenix rising from the ashes already has the mark of death upon it. Likewise, when the nuclear dyad of Cormac McCarthy's *The Road* makes an appearance in *Zone One*, Mark Spitz is wary of its kinship and attachment structures:

> A parent-child combo might pop up at the crest of the old country road, wan and wary, and Mark Spitz shrank from these, no matter how well outfitted they were. Parenthood made grown-ups unpredictable. They were paranoid he wanted to rape or eat their offspring... they possessed the valuables, and it hobbled their reasoning.[53]

Mark Spitz models from the outside the doubts of the boy in *The Road*, who is frequently dubious about his father's assertions that they are the "good guys" who are "carrying the fire." For all his apparent everydayness, Mark Spitz has a "knack for the apocalypse." It is not just his practical survival skills; his insight into who is already dead means he is always primed to deploy them. This is a capability he has brought forward from his prior life and now flourishes as an early-warning system in his present circumstances: "He was dragging a corpse out of a laundry joint on Chambers Street down in the Zone when he realized that the voice

---

52. Whitehead (2011) 17, 124–25.
53. Whitehead (2011) 114. Hicks (2016) 111 notes the resemblance to McCarthy's postapocalyptic pair.

admonishing him to ditch the survivors he'd hooked up with, warning him away from others, was an echo of his relationship-snuffing voice. They are the lost, they are the dead, it is time to leave."⁵⁴ Mark Spitz's visionary predation thrives on the sacrificial offering of others. Ontological attunement is the ground of his survival skills, and this attunement requires constant testing and careful maintenance if it is to continue to function as the refusal of shared life with what is not truly or fully alive that keeps him safe.

Like *Zone One*, Octavia Butler's *The Parable of the Sower* takes place in a future much of which is already here, a southern California of walled estates and servants' shacks that is an exaggeration of present conditions rather than a radically different social reality. In this world, survivalism means "getting ready to survive it," preparing to "make a life afterward," so that you can do more than just "get batted around by crazy people, desperate people, things, and leaders who don't know what they're doing." Prepping for a gradualist apocalypse is compared to life in postplague medieval Europe, and in its early stages the project of Butler's protagonist, Lauren Oya Olamina, is continuous with the ways in which other postapocalyptic fiction sets its sights on the historical record, both for what is needed to survive and for its visions of what postapocalyptic life might look like. As in *Into the Forest*, for example, the novel stages a debate around the idea that "books aren't going to save us," the outcome of which is that some books might actually be helpful, including "some fiction," and whatever records remain of the plant knowledge of the California Indians, who lived without the fossil fuel civilization that is ebbing away and whose benefits are mostly unavailable to poor people anyway.⁵⁵

---

54. Whitehead (2011) 194–95.
55. Butler (2017) 66–69. It is difficult not to see Butler herself in the grandmother who left Olamina "a whole bookcase of old science fiction novels" (132). See the interviews with Butler in Francis (2010) 10, 15, 85 for her long-standing interest in anthropology and Deep History, and for her understanding of the persistent

Where Olamina differs from the protagonists of other postapocalyptic fiction is in her eventual realization that to arrive at an inhabitable future, she and the other survivors need a new ontology with which to extricate themselves from the ways of understanding that are available to them in the present. This is what she calls Earthseed, a series of verse reflections that punctuate the novel as chapter headings, where they mark the increase in her own attunement to this project but also become an agent within the narrative, as she begins to conceive of them not just as a way of capturing her own understanding of reality but as a way of extricating others from the limits of the present: "I'll use these verses to pry them loose from the rotting past."[56]

Olamina compares Earthseed to her father's readings from the Bible: "Gentle, brief verses that might take hold of him without his realizing it and live in his memory without his intending that they should. Bits of the Bible had done that to me, staying with me even after I stopped believing."[57] Butler's belief that religion could be harnessed as a motive force for social goods has been amply documented with respect to her work as a whole.[58] With regard to the *Parable* novels specifically, she claimed to be leveraging the fact that "there are no human communities without religion."[59] Earthseed consists of fragmentary, nontotalizing ontological reflections that are nonetheless a centripetal agent in community formation by virtue of a psychoactive power that is independent of dogmatic or even didactic intentions, like her father's Bible verses.

The form in which Olamina and her father metabolize the Bible—arresting its narrative movement and breaking down its authority into short, aphoristic fragments that might be poems, songs,

---

relationship between historical fiction and survivalist group ideology in the conception of the second *Parable* novel (114–15).

56. Butler (2017) 89.
57. Butler (2017) 206.
58. Butler in Francis (2010) 121–22, 174–75; Canavan (2016) 123–51.
59. Butler in Francis (2010) 174.

or rhythmic prose—and the way this metabolization operates to produce shared life echo the work of early Greek ontologists like Heraclitus. In *Parts of Animals*, Aristotle exhorts his readers not to turn away from the study of even the most humble life-forms, "since in all natural things there is something of the marvelous." As part of this exhortation, he includes an anecdote about how a group of visitors who were keen to meet Heraclitus once called on him at his house. Noticing their disappointment when they found him warming himself at the kitchen stove, he invited them to join him: "Come in; don't be afraid; there are gods even here."[60]

Heraclitus's visitors are strangers or foreigners, *xenous*. Aristotle's reminder that all living beings are worthy of our attention is also a protreptic toward shared life in the practice of ontology. Different people, especially if they are from different cultures, will have different kinds of acquaintance with living beings as a whole. Beyond even this consideration, different people are naturally drawn to different kinds of natural entities, and it is for this reason that ontology works best as a communitarian practice. Individual participants may become better attuned to the ways of the cosmos in the particular local manifestation to which they themselves belong by attending to the forms of belonging that seem natural to others. By doing ontology together, they are less likely to be victimized by traditional beliefs and dogmatic philosophies.

I do not mean to suggest that Octavia Butler's conception of Earthseed was influenced by pre-Socratic philosophy or Aristotle's account of it, only that these provide a useful model for understanding how Earthseed works as a parareligious community-building project. Earthseed is not simply a text or a set of beliefs. It is a practice—an ongoing commitment to shared reflection that involves participants in a common ontological project that is not hermeneutic in nature, since it aims not at conclusive understanding in the present, but rather at further rounds of ontological speculation and invention—a form of culturecraft, if you like.

60. Aristotle, *Parts of Animals* 1.5.645a.

The future will not be apprehended all at once in the form of a systematic philosophy. It will emerge from the past like burls from a nurse log, which nourishes the green shoots of new thinking before it is supplanted by them. The one constant injunction of Earthseed is to recognize, enable, and attend to the work of change in oneself and the cosmos.[61]

Like the pre-Socratic writings, Earthseed is shareable in the precise sense that it is something you are meant to do to and for yourself, but with others for company. By doing the work of Earthseed, you become Earthseed. As Olamina and her survivor group make their way north from Los Angeles among the streams of migrants heading toward the greener, better-watered lands of northern California, Oregon, and the Canadian coast—"a broad river of people walking west on the freeway"[62]—she gathers new companions in whose company she acquires a range of postapocalyptic capabilities: marksmanship, butchery, how to disguise a campsite, and so forth. But whereas Mark Spitz shared his ontology only with those he had already learned to trust, for Olamina, a willingness to engage with her ontology is the condition of trust. Anyone wishing to join her survival group must engage with Earthseed first, whatever other capabilities they are bringing to the table.

For Olamina and her group, the goal is Cape Mendocino in Humboldt County, where her partner Bankole owns land on which they will found the community of Acorn, which is intended as the societal enactment of Earthseed's ontology. The reader experiences both Earthseed's necessity and its difficulty from the perspective of the would-be settlers. While they admire Olamina and respect her survival skills, all of them, including

---

61. Butler (2017) 89; cf. Stillman (2003) 23–27.
62. Butler (2017) 182. Like Whitehead, she insists on the image of the "ever-flowing river of people" (222), the "rivers of people flowing north" (326–27) that are a "river of the poor" (230) bearing all manner of carts and other such Hesiodic transportation along with them as the additional freight of this "usual human river" (264).

Bankole—who is the community doctor as well as the donor of the land on which Acorn is founded—experience doubts, on occasions rising to violent aversion, about both the content of Earthseed and the requirement to engage with it as a condition of community membership. For while dogmatic assent to its principles is not required, participation in the communal practice of reflecting on its teachings is mandatory, as is a commitment not to practice other beliefs out of respect for Earthseed, so that they will wither away beside it, like the other seeds in the biblical parable. Admission requires submission, and if most readers, like most would-be community members, do eventually buy in, it is because they are offered a vision of how it works in practice that overcomes the intellectual and emotional discomfort of the buy-in itself.

In the second of the *Parable* novels, *The Parable of the Talents*, narrated by Olamina's daughter, Butler drastically falsifies this vision of assent with a retrospective perspective from within Olamina's own family. Her daughter calls her mother's teachings "damned Earthseed" and claims they carried no more conviction in the period narrated in the first novel than anyone else's dreams. Every survivor, she claims, "used dreams—our fantasies—to sustain us through hard times." The only difference is that Olamina's have been instrumentalized in the meantime by a society that is not noticeably different than the one from which she claimed to be freeing her adherents.[63] The other members of Acorn, we glean, submitted out of a desire for the security it represented.

Olamina is now a wealthy, self-absorbed celebrity. The spaceship that represents the culmination of her ambitions for Earthseed is named the *Christopher Columbus*. If we do not simply dismiss her daughter's rewriting of the earlier novel as resentment at her mother's neglect of her, what are we to make of the circumscription of the first book by the second? Is *The Parable of the*

63. Butler (2017) 13, 57.

Talents an accelerated, self-authored version of the subversive rewrite of a canonical predecessor, like J. M. Coetzee's *Foe*?[64]

Gerry Canavan has argued that Butler's thought in the *Parable* novels is less dialectical than antinomic. There is a "constitutional contradiction" in these works, a "stalled or arrested dialectic" she is unable to move beyond, and he points to the survival of the species versus the misery of the individual as one form of the antinomy by which "the critique of neoliberalism in the Parables books produces not the opposite of neoliberal atomism but rather a *radically* neoliberal subject—something more neoliberal than neoliberalism itself."[65]

Is, then, the reframing of the prosocial ontology of *The Parable of the Sower* in *The Parable of the Talents* further evidence of the stall out to which Canavan points? The *Parable* novels were originally conceived as the prequel to a story of space settlement that was never written. The adaptive ontology of Earthseed was meant to prepare the ground for a decisive remaking of human capabilities beyond the earth itself. Living in space would be so difficult it would require a "new idea of human solidarity," as human beings would have to work together to an extent unprecedented in human history, and perhaps even beyond the limits of existing human biology, with what Butler believed were its inherent hierarchical biases. Nonetheless, what "the outer space frontier" offered was a chance "not to *abolish* human nature but perhaps to temporarily suspend it." The colonization of space would be a chance to start over, in circumstances "whose radical hardship would offer a chance to build new practices of solidarity and collective life."[66]

We have noted the return of the frontier, and of frontier spirit, in Colson Whitehead's *Zone One*. On the posthuman frontier, regeneration through violence is legitimate once again. Frontierspersons

---

64. On the critical intentions and fictional strategies of such rewrites, see Doležel (1998) 199–226.

65. Canavan (2016) 134, 143.

66. Canavan (2016) 126.

have the opportunity to really live, to live to the max in fact, among the "slow desperadoes and fellow sheriffs, meting out justice in the territory." Butler herself believed that starting over was the only way of moving forward, and that starting over meant finding a new frontier: "The best way to do something else is to go someplace else where the demands on us will be different. Not because we are going to go someplace else and change ourselves, but because we will go someplace else and be forced to change."[67] There is no hope that human beings might produce for themselves a dialectical resolution of what afflicts them in the here and now. The only hope is for an apocalyptic leap beyond it, into what might transform them from the outside in. A return to the frontier is willed regression, going backward to look forward, finding the place where the road should have ended, where you wish your ancestors had stopped.

For postapocalyptic fiction generally, something has to happen to human beings if they are to exit the stall of contemporary possibilities. For postapocalyptic fiction whose understanding of human capabilities is modeled on the anthropological record, a stable species concept subtends its understanding of the capabilities recovered through the apocalyptic event. There is no sense in turning to the speculative Neolithic for a vision of the future unless you believe that human bodies preserve the powers of their distant ancestors. In this vision, postapocalyptic time is the flowering of latent, transhistorical human capabilities.

But there is also a flowering that can't be shown. In E. M. Forster's "The Machine Stops," a global technological failure ushers in a new age of survival for whoever is able to escape the all-providing machine that has hitherto serviced their needs for food, shelter, and entertainment. On the far side of this machine for living is a Rousseauian recovery of the body's abrogated feeling of existence: "The sun against the body—it was for that they wept in chief; the centuries of wrong against the muscles and the nerves, and those five portals by which we can alone apprehend—glozing it over

---

67. Butler in Francis (2010) 71. Cf. Canavan (2016) 138.

with talk of evolution, until the body was white pap, the home of ideas as colourless, last sloshy stirrings of a spirit that had grasped the stars."[68]

Forster's story models the relationship between body and mind in Rousseau's speculative anthropology. The body is "the home of ideas," and not until it has new occupations will its ideas be anything but colorless. The mind this body houses is likewise unaware that its listlessness is a consequence of its body's disoccupation. But Forster does not take the next step and give the content of postapocalyptic mind as an expansive consciousness of shared life with living beings as a whole as this content emerges in Jean Hegland's *Into the Forest*, or Rousseau's more circumscribed recovery of the sentiment of existence in *Reveries of the Solitary Walker*.

Hegland and Rousseau are retrospective in their attention to the anthropological record. Forster, like Butler, is a prospector. The refusal of dialectical resolution is not a refusal of politics but an acknowledgment of its limits. Marronage off the earth, like marronage on the earth, requires open spaces in which to enact its freedom. Leaving a gap for the flowering that can't be shown means believing there is somewhere this flowering can happen. Taking the suspension of human nature seriously means believing there is a place where it could be rebooted. If there are human capabilities not subtended by a stable species concept, they need a site to emerge. If Olamina's ontological imagination has been co-opted by business as usual, this does not mean her vision of a new life among the stars is a lie. Only that it can't be shown, even by her creator.

---

68. Forster (2001) 123.

CONCLUSION

Landscape with Figures

TO THE THEORY of marronage that is so vital to postapocalyptic fiction, there corresponds the figure of the maroon, a being of both fiction and history. Postapocalyptic fiction invokes various historical forms of life to shape its vision of postapocalyptic sociality, but the maroon is common to them all as a figure of the passage from one form of life to another. Whether in Richard Jefferies's *After London* or Octavia Butler's *The Parable of the Sower*, the protagonists move from a world of unfreedom into open spaces beyond the polis walls. Others may occupy this space before them, but after the apocalypse, there is enough room for everyone. Here they come to a new understanding of their own capabilities, and this experience affords them a new vision of the collective—Felix Aquila's pastoral tribalism in England's southland, or Lauren Oya Olamina's Acorn community in northern California.

In conclusion, I want to explore the overlap between the postapocalyptic figure of the maroon and two figures of the relationship between freedom and catastrophe in mid-twentieth-century political theory: Ernst Jünger's forest fleer and Carl Schmitt's cosmopartisan. In *The Forest Passage*, Jünger's post–World War II reflection on the possibilities for freedom in the modern bureaucratic state, he proposes "forest flight" as a theory of freedom and the "forest fleer" as the figure who enacts it.[1] As Russell Berman notes in his introduction to the English translation, Jünger's critical account of state penetration into previously sacrosanct areas of private life via health care, well-being initiatives, and other such philanthropic endeavors anticipates Michel Foucault's better-known theorization of biopolitics.[2] And on the constructive side, there are many points of contact between his forest fleer, the New World maroon, and the protagonists of postapocalyptic fiction.

In *On the Marble Cliffs* (1939), his speculative fiction of midcentury European tyranny, Jünger evinces a detailed knowledge of fugitivity in the colonial Caribbean.[3] Like the maroon, the forest fleer's freedom is in the first instance negative—a refusal to participate in regular forms of political life or to assent to an idea of freedom beyond what is enacted in fugitivity itself. Withdrawal comes first, because the "new conception of freedom" needed for the times is nowhere at hand, one that would have nothing to do with the washed-out civic associations of the word "freedom" today. Moving beyond Rousseau's claim that modernity entails the loss of capabilities grounded in the individual body and its powers, Jünger argues that the modern state's care for its subjects entails a loss of ethical capability too. The new conception of freedom envisages not just the recovery of bodily capabilities but that this recovery will lead to new forms of ethicality: "The individual still

---

1. "Forest fleer" and "forest flight" are Joachim Neugroschel's renditions of Jünger's "*Waldgänger*" and "*Waldgang*" in his translation of Jünger's postapocalyptic novel *Eumeswil*. Thomas Friese, translator of *The Forest Passage*, prefers "forest rebel" and "forest passage" because "the word 'flight' has a connotation of running away from normal reality, the choice of a weaker, not a stronger, individual," Jünger (2013) x–xi. I have retained Neugroschel's terms because of their resonance with marronage and fugitivity.

2. Jünger (2013) xx. Jünger does not figure in, for example, Rose (2007).

3. See, for example, the pursuit of fugitives with the mastiffs used to hunt escaped Caribbean slaves, Jünger (1947) 98–99, which is so terrifyingly imagined in Chamoiseau (2018).

possesses organs in which more wisdom lies than in the entire [state or party] organization."[4]

Like Dicaearchus, Jünger claims that the memory of what human beings are capable of is preserved in the stratified layers of folktale and poetry, in contrast to the inert existence of the past in our own Iron Age historicism. The contemporary turn to the anthropological record is a sign of hope for the "radiation age," and the most urgent question that this age poses is how we should orient ourselves to its apocalyptic potential: "Should we count on catastrophe?" Is apocalypse the necessary horizon for the new conception of freedom, because it is only postapocalyptically that we can imagine what it envisages emerging?[5]

It is in light of this question that the forest fleer's overlap with the figure of the maroon is shown to be only partial. In his prewar prose collection *The Adventurous Heart*, Jünger cites the same maxim of Cicero on Bias of Priene that Rousseau repurposes in *The Discourse on Inequality*: "The wanderer, like Bias, 'takes everything he owns with himself.'"[6] So, too, his forest fleer carries his ethical capabilities with him at all times as an inalienable possession that only requires activation. What he accesses in fugitivity is a "latent supra-temporal essence" of humankind that is available to anyone anywhere. "Ostracized, condemned, fleeing," the forest fleer "encounters himself anew," but what he encounters in himself is an "invulnerable core": "the being that sustains and feeds the individual phenomenon in time."[7] Catastrophes "must be practiced for," but they are not necessary. The forest fleer lacks the plasticity of the maroon, who must go elsewhere in order to be remade there.

In *Theory of the Partisan*, Carl Schmitt comes to a reckoning of his own with Jünger's question in *The Forest Passage*: "Should we

---

4. Jünger (2013) 13, 23, 36, 46.
5. Jünger (2013) 43, 77.
6. Jünger (2012) 89. Cf. Rousseau (1997) 135 and Cicero, *Paradoxes of the Stoics*, 1.8: *Omnia mea mecum porto*.
7. Jünger (2013) 24, 67, 48, 81–82.

count on catastrophe?" Schmitt theorizes the figure of the partisan as an outcome of the increasingly ideological nature of global conflict from the Napoleonic wars to colonial Algeria and Indo-China. Like the pirate, the partisan is a figure of local resistance to global ideology, but whereas the pirate acts anomically, for pure personal gain, the partisan enacts a relationship of defensive attachment to the terrain he occupies, which Schmitt calls "telluric." The pirate is a figure of mobility, the partisan a figure in a landscape.

From this perspective of total global conflict, Schmitt reflects on the possibilities for reinhabitation of the earth in the aftermath of nuclear war and the related need for extraterrestrial colonization. On one hand, a "new type of partisan" might emerge to reoccupy an earth largely voided of its human population. On the other, weapons of mass destruction might devastate the earth so thoroughly that "a new type of space-appropriation" is required. The contrast between these forms of life is only superficial. A postnuclear earth would resemble an alien planet, and the difficulties a pioneer group would face would be similar in either scenario: "The famous astronauts and cosmonauts, who formerly were only propaganda stars of the mass media (press, radio, television), will have the opportunity to become cosmopirates, even perhaps to morph into cosmopartisans."[8]

Schmitt is doubtful that these extraterrestrial and postapocalyptic occupations can emerge in the first instance in any other way than as an extension of state power: "Only he who ostensibly dominates an earth that has becomes so tiny will be able to appropriate and to utilize new spaces."[9] But on the far side of this pessimism, in the conjuncture of extraterrestriality and apocalyptic clearing, one can hear the call of open space that is the animating power of maroon fugitivity—Octavia Butler's going someplace else and being remade there. The cosmopartisan is the figure of a new form of life. For on what planet can we imagine that she

8. Schmitt (2007) 79–80.
9. Schmitt (2007) 80.

would not be transformed by the capabilities her new occupation elicits?

At the end of Margaret Atwood's *MaddAddam* trilogy, the conflict between pirate and partisan is decisively terminated in favor of the latter with the execution of the survivalists, whose only motivations are the rapacious acquisition of consumer goods and the pursuit of pleasure, typically sadistic in nature. A new era of political relations comes into being with the unexpected signing of compacts between the human survivors, their posthuman replacements, and the transgenic Pigoons. With each group now settled in its own part of the terrain, the period of maroon self-discovery is at an end. Treaties regulate ethnic coexistence and are policed by their various signatories.

The convergence between the figures of postapocalyptic fiction and the figures of political theory is clearly legible here. But what does such convergence mean? Who are these figures, and what is the nature of the appeal to them, whether in postapocalyptic fiction itself or in political theory that looks to catastrophe for its vision of a common human future?

Linda Zerilli has argued for the importance of the figure of woman in Western political theory. In contrast to actual flesh-and-blood historical women, woman is a fictive being invested with enough local detail to be credible, but with gaps, voids, inconsistencies, and anachronisms that allow for imaginative projection on the part of theory's readers. The figure of woman allows "spaces to be organized, protean energies to be harnessed." An imaginary future constellates itself around the hopes and fears it stages in personal form. It allows an impasse of political meaning to be circumvented by affording a vision of what comes next.[10]

It is the mixed ontology of the figure of woman that allows it to do the work of constellating a future form of life around itself. The figure is a historical and affective bricolage that invites its readers

10. Zerilli (1994) 2–5, 141–42.

to galvanize its potential with their own imaginative energy, to make it perform on the stage of a future that will succeed the world they know. The figures of postapocalyptic fiction likewise emerge from a mixed ontology of historical piecework and affects toward the present. Robinson Crusoe is already such a hybrid—part Alexander Selkirk, part Greek tragic hero, part Defoe's invention, but also, irreducibly, something else as well: a figure only thinly realized as a fictional being precisely because he inhabits a world in which human beings have rediscovered capabilities of which they are only dimly aware, with the forms of mentation that accompany them—a figural gestalt that can only be opaque to the reader.

In his account of the long history of the Robinsonade, Istvan Csicsery-Ronay argues that, as the specific conditions in which Defoe's novel was legible as the "bourgeois epic of technical world-construction" have receded, its diegetic agents have become increasingly figural. We no longer encounter a Crusoe and a Friday in their fictional singularity but the Handy Man, the Fertile Corpse, the Willing Slave, the Shadow Mage, the Tool/Text, and the Wife at Home. The increasing emphasis on figuration enacts at the level of world-building the thematics of freedom from the constraints of a particular kind of world that is the foundational fictional event of the Robinsonade. Figuration exposes the mixed ontology of the form, clarifying its futural orientation.[11]

In *When Species Meet*, Donna Haraway likewise invokes eighteenth-century usage of the word figure as "chimerical vision" as a way of populating a possible future with beings sourced from a mix of ontological origins:

> Figures help me grapple inside the flesh of mortal world-making entanglements that I call contact zones. . . . Figures collect the people through their invitation to inhabit the corporeal

---

11. Csicsery-Ronay (2008) 225. Cf. Csicsery-Ronay (2003) 232, where the work of Negri and Hardt is used in an explicitly figural way as a "a tool for understanding contemporary geopolitical mythology" and the challenges to it that sf is able to mount in this figural mode.

story told in their lineaments. Figures are not representations or didactic illustrations, but rather material-semiotic nodes or knots in which diverse bodies and meanings coshape one another. For me, figures have always been where the biological and literary or artistic come together with all of the force of lived reality.... The partners do not precede the meeting.[12]

Figures make futures because of their hybrid ontology. They are agents of sympoiesis, of coming into being through shared becoming.[13]

Sophie Lewis has criticized Haraway's recourse to the figure, and the disavowed apocalyptic figure of H. P. Lovecraft's Cthulhu in *Staying with the Trouble*, in particular, for its occluded catastrophism. Haraway, Lewis claims, is unwilling to acknowledge the human costs of her desire for a reduction in the human population espoused in the name of sympoietic relationships with the companion species that make us human.[14] If there is a silence at the heart of the future, where is the act of contrition, the dance for the dead?

But the figure of postapocalyptic fiction is not an agent of critique, a way of realizing a future we have in mind for ourselves. Just the opposite, in fact. Like the herdsman of pastoral poetry, its role is to occupy a space until the real world of becoming is available again. The maroon is prosocial but a figure of transit. Holding open a space for becoming is what allows us to go on, but with the emergence of politics as such, the time of the maroon is at an end.

12. Haraway (2008) 4.

13. Cf. the invocation of *figures* explicitly in connection with sympoiesis and speculative fabulation in Haraway (2016) 133: "Attached to ongoing pasts, they bring each other forward in thick presents and still possible futures."

14. Lewis (2017) 5–6. She claims that while figural thinking has been a staple of Haraway's work since the 1980s, the more recent instances—"the 'modest witness'; the coyote; the trickster; FemaleMan; the Surrogate, the 'companion species'; Oncomouse™; and since 2014, 'string figures' and 'chthonic ones'"—are both "far less popular, and far less politically generative" than the Cyborg of the earlier Cyborg Manifesto.

An aura of reticence surrounds this figure. As Jerome McGann observes, the "future perfect temporality" of *Blake* points directly from the past to a future not yet achieved, not yet even imaginable in detail.[15] Or as the mission priest in D'Arcy McNickle's *Wind from an Enemy Sky* reflects: "The Indian has always remained beyond our reach, just beyond our reach. He is always slipping away into the distance.... He is both opposed to us and trying to escape from us—as if he could escape!"[16]

The figure of postapocalyptic fiction must bide its time, until the time within it can flower again. Until that time, it is essentially fugitive, evanescent, maroon:

> In its distancing from the temporal present, the location of the romantic space appears as something past, and indeed as one colored through *ressentiment* against the current situation. This distancing from the local present is represented as flight from a space entirely secured and saturated by consciousness, and that is why the number of romantic landscapes shrinks in direct proportion to the advance of technology, the most acute instrument of consciousness. Yesterday, perhaps, such landscapes could still be found "far away in Turkey," or Spain and Greece, today in the jungle belt around the equator or the ice caps of the poles, but tomorrow the last white specks on this strange map of human longing will have vanished.[17]

Jünger would come to think better of his dismissal of Romantic longing for the outside, and we should too. The map can always be unfilled, the gaps restored, and reticence is a welcome gesture in the direction of this unknowing.

Once upon a time there was a city in southern Illinois called Cahokia. It was built quickly, and at the height of its brief period of

---

15. Delany (2017) xvi–xvii.
16. McNickle (1988) 51–52.
17. Jünger (2017) 31.

flourishing, around 1100 CE, its population was greater than that of London. The inhabitants were distributed between a central administrative and ceremonial zone and a constellation of satellite communities, each devoted to a specialized manufacturing activity. For this was a city of centralized urban planning of a kind North America had not seen before. And then, just as suddenly as it was built, Cahokia was abandoned. The terrain was eventually reoccupied, but the city itself was never rebuilt. Not until the last decades of the eighteenth century did a city appear on North American soil that surpassed it in size.[18]

The Cahokians left no records. We do not know why they abandoned their city. Later occupants of the terrain claimed to have no knowledge of the huge earthen pyramids that rise toward the horizon out of the Mississippi floodplain. And if we believe Hawthorne's story of the Great Sagamore, the Cahokians would have remained silent too. No one wants instructions on the good life; we want to find out how to live it for ourselves. Cahokia shows us something, but it does not tell us anything. We can only speculate.

Some genres come to an end through no fault of their own. On an earth whose last white specks have been mapped—Google mapped, even—it is hard to see much of a future for mysterious islands and their people. Extraterrestrial worlds and the apocalypse are what we are left with. Native American histories abound with stories of enigmatic injunctions to seek out new forms of life in hitherto unknown places. The Crow separate from the Hidatsa to seek out a tobacco plant in the mountains to the west of the Missouri floodplain, their ancestral homeland. The Anishinaabeg set off for a place where food grows on water.

Indigenous storytelling is rich in forking paths, moments when life could have been expected to keep on keeping on but instead branched off in some unanticipated direction. In *The Way to Rainy Mountain*, N. Scott Momaday talks about the Kiowa coming into

---

18. On the "big bang" at Cahokia and the city's mysterious demise, see Pauketat (2009).

their story with the advent of the horse, a history no one could have seen coming, but which they made their own through their will to imagine a new form of life for themselves. Such stories are unlike the linear narratives of Western history, in which life advances in a predictable sequence of developments or, in the case of the postapocalyptic glissade, their sudden, but no less predictable, reversal.

Indigenous stories are not tales of environmental determinism. The figures of the story respond to what faces them in ways they choose for themselves. For this reason, they are stories of resilience and hope. Events come from outside, but the form of life they enable is freely chosen. Postapocalyptic fiction is also about choosing a different form of life. The apocalyptic event may ultimately be only a necessary fiction that allows its readers to choose, as the Kiowa or Cahokians chose. This would be another reason to see it as a cheerful genre, a way of courage in resignation, or resignation in courage, like the culturecraft of the ancient sages.

In *Always Coming Home,* Ursula Le Guin speculates that "destruction destroys itself," and we might also speculate that there are more or less convulsive forms in which this destruction can happen, as the destroyers are more or less reflective about their destructiveness. Pandora's question seems like a good one to pose to the Cahokians:

> In leaving progress to the machines, in letting technology go forward on its own terms and selecting from it, with what seems to us excessive caution, modesty, or restraint, the limited though completely adequate implements of their cultures, is it possible that in thus opting not to move "forward" or not only "forward," these people did in fact succeed in living in human history, with energy, liberty, and grace?[19]

---

19. Le Guin (2019) 447–48.

WORKS CITED

Fiction and Poetry

Atwood, M. 2004. *Oryx and Crake*. New York: Anchor Books.
Atwood, M. 2010. *The Year of the Flood*. New York: Anchor Books.
Atwood, M. 2014. *MaddAddam*. New York: Anchor Books.
Auster, P. 1987. *In the Country of Last Things*. New York: Penguin Books.
Bellamy, E. 2007. *Looking Backward*. Oxford: Oxford University Press.
Beresford, J. D. 2013. *Goslings*. Brooklyn: HiLo Books.
Brin, D. 1985. *The Postman*. New York: Bantam Books.
Butler, O. E. 2017. *The Parable of the Sower*. New York: Seven Stories Press.
Butler, O. E. 2017. *The Parable of the Talents*. New York: Seven Stories Press.
Butler, S. 1970. *Erewhon*. New York: Penguin Books.
Chamoiseau, P. 2018. *Slave Old Man*. New York: New Press.
Christopher, J. 2016. *The Death of Grass*. n.p.: SYLE Press.
Clare, J. 2003. *"I Am": The Selected Poetry of John Clare*. New York: Farrar, Straus and Giroux.
Clare, J. 2004. *Major Works*. Oxford: Oxford University Press.
Clare, J. 2006. *The Shepherd's Calendar*. Manchester: Carcanet Press.
Collier, J. 1933. *Full Circle: A Tale*. New York: D. Appleton (published in the UK as *Tom's A-Cold*).
Crace, J. 2007. *The Pesthouse*. New York: Vintage Books.
Delany, M. R. 2017. *Blake; or, The Huts of America: A Corrected Edition*. Cambridge, MA: Harvard University Press.
Doyle, A. C. 2001. *The Poison Belt: Being an Account of Another Amazing Adventure of Professor Challenger*. Lincoln: University of Nebraska Press.
Forster, E. M. 2001. *Selected Stories*. New York: Penguin Books.
Frank, P. 2005. *Alas, Babylon*. New York: Harper Books.
Hamilton, C. 2013. *Theodore Savage*. Brooklyn: HiLo Books.
Hawthorne, N. 1977. *The Elixir of Life Manuscripts*. Columbus: Ohio State University Press.

Hegland, J. 1998. *Into the Forest*. New York: Dial Press.
Hesiod. 2018. *Theogony. Works and Days. Testimonia.* Cambridge, MA: Harvard University Press (Loeb Classical Library 57).
Jefferies, R. 2017. *After London; or, Wild England*. Edinburgh: Edinburgh University Press.
Kingsnorth, P. 2013. *The Wake*. Minneapolis: Graywolf Press.
Le Guin, U. K. 2019. *Always Coming Home: Author's Expanded Edition*. New York: Library of America.
Lessing, D. 1974. *The Memoirs of a Survivor*. New York: Vintage Books.
Matheson, R. 1995. *I Am Legend*. New York: Orb Editions.
McCarthy, C. 2006. *The Road*. New York: Vintage Books.
McNickle, D. 1988. *Wind from an Enemy Sky*. Albuquerque: University of New Mexico Press.
McNickle, D. 2003. *The Surrounded*. Albuquerque: University of New Mexico Press.
Melville, H. 1990. *The Confidence-Man*. New York: Penguin Books.
Mitchell, J. L. 1989. *Gay Hunter*. Edinburgh: Polygon.
Mitchell, J. L. 1999. *Three Go Back*. Edinburgh: Polygon.
Morris, W. 1993. *News from Nowhere and Other Writings*. New York: Penguin Books.
See, C. 1996. *Golden Days*. Berkeley: University of California Press.
Shanks, E. 2012. *The People of the Ruins*. Brooklyn: HiLo Books.
Shelley, M. 1994. *The Last Man*. Oxford: Oxford University Press.
Shiel, M. P. 2012. *The Purple Cloud*. New York: Penguin Books.
Shute, N. 2010. *On the Beach*. New York: Vintage Books.
Stapledon, O. 1997. *An Olaf Stapledon Reader*. Syracuse, NY: Syracuse University Press.
Stapledon, O. 2008. *Last and First Men*. Mineola, NY: Dover Books.
Stapledon, O. 2008. *Star Maker*. Mineola, NY: Dover Books.
Stewart, G. R. 2006. *Earth Abides*. New York: Del Ray Books.
Theroux, M. 2010. *Far North*. New York: Picador.
Thoreau, H. D. 1991. *Walden*. New York: Library of America.
Welch, J. 1974. *Winter in the Blood*. New York: Penguin Books.
Whitehead, C. 2011. *Zone One*. New York: Doubleday.

Theory, Criticism, History

Bennett, J. 1994. *Thoreau's Nature: Ethics, Politics, and the Wild*. Thousand Oaks, CA: Sage.
Berger, J. 1999. *After the End: Representations of Post-Apocalypse*. Minneapolis: University of Minnesota Press.

Buell, L. 1996. *The Environmental Imagination*. Cambridge, MA: Harvard University Press.

Buell, L. 2008. "The Unkillable Dream of the Great American Novel: *Moby-Dick* as Test Case." *American Literary History* 20.1–2: 132–55.

Canavan, G. 2016. *Octavia E. Butler*. Urbana: University of Illinois Press.

Canuel, M. 1998. "Acts, Rules, and *The Last Man*." *Nineteenth-Century Literature* 53.2: 147–70.

Cavell, S. 1992. *The Senses of* Walden. Chicago: University of Chicago Press.

Clastres, P. 1989. *Society against the State*. New York: Zone Books.

Clute, J., and Nicholls, P. 1999. *The Encyclopedia of Science Fiction*. London: Palgrave Macmillan.

Cooper, S. 2019. "Speculative Fiction, Ecocriticism, and the Wanderings of Odysseus." *Ramus* 48.2: 95–126.

Csicsery-Ronay, I., Jr. 2003. "Science Fiction and Empire." *Science Fiction Studies* 30: 231–45.

Csicsery-Ronay, I., Jr. 2008. *The Seven Beauties of Science Fiction*. Middletown, CT: Wesleyan University Press.

Curran, S. 1986. *Poetic Form and British Romanticism*. Oxford: Oxford University Press.

Curtis, C. P. 2010. *Postapocalyptic Fiction and the Social Contract: "We'll Not Go Home Again."* Lanham, MD: Lexington Books.

Doležel, L. 1998. *Heterocosmica: Fiction and Possible Worlds*. Baltimore: Johns Hopkins University Press.

Douglass, F. 2003. *My Bondage and My Freedom*. New York: Penguin.

Ebbatson, J. R. 1977. "Visions of Wild England: William Morris and Richard Jefferies." *Journal of William Morris Studies* 3.3: 12–29.

Fate, T. M. 2011. *Cabin Fever*. Boston: Beacon Press.

Fortenbaugh, W. W., and Schütrumpf, E. 2001. *Dicaearchus of Messana*. London: Routledge (Rutgers University Studies in Classical Humanities).

Francis, C. 2010. *Conversations with Octavia Butler*. Jackson: University of Mississippi Press.

Friedrich, P. 2008. *The Gita within* Walden. Albany: State University of New York Press.

Frost, M. 2017. "Introduction." In *After London; or Wild England*. Edinburgh: Edinburgh University Press: vii–xlvi.

Ghosh, A. 2017. *The Great Derangement: Climate Change and the Unthinkable*. Chicago: University of Chicago Press.

Glissant, É. 1997. *Poetics of Relation*. Ann Arbor: University of Michigan Press.

Gollin, R. K. 2005. "Estranged Allegiances in Hawthorne's Unfinished Romances." In *Hawthorne and the Real: Bicentennial Essays*, ed. M. Bell. Columbus: Ohio State University Press: 159–80.

Haraway, D. J. 2008. *When Species Meet*. Minneapolis: University of Minnesota Press.
Haraway, D. J. 2016. *Staying with the Trouble: Making Kin in the Chthulucene*. Durham, NC: Duke University Press.
Hay, J. 2017. *Postapocalyptic Fantasies in Antebellum American Literature*. Cambridge: Cambridge University Press.
Heffernan, T. 2008. *Post-Apocalyptic Culture: Modernism, Postmodernism, and the Twentieth-Century Novel*. Toronto: University of Toronto Press.
Heise, U. 2015. "What's the Matter with Dystopia?" www.publicbooks.org/whats-the-matter-with-dystopia.
Hicks, H. J. 2016. *The Post-Apocalyptic Novel in the Twenty-First Century: Modernity beyond Salvage*. New York: Palgrave Macmillan.
Hoberek, A. 2011. "Cormac McCarthy and the Aesthetics of Exhaustion." *American Literary History* 23.3: 483–99.
Hoberek, A. 2012. "Living with PASD." *Contemporary Literature* 53.2: 406–413.
Holmes, B. 2013. "The Poetic Logic of Negative Exceptionalism in Lucretius, Book Five." In *Lucretius: Poetry, Philosophy, Science*, ed. D. Lehoux, A. D. Morrison, A. Sharrock. Oxford: Oxford University Press: 153–91.
Horden, P., and Purcell, N. 2000. *The Corrupting Sea: A Study of Mediterranean History*. Oxford: Blackwell.
Horn, E. 2014. "The Last Man: The Birth of Modern Apocalypse in Jean Paul, John Martin, and Lord Byron." In *Catastrophes: A History and Theory of an Operative Concept*, ed. N. Lebovic and A. Killen. Berlin: De Gruyter: 55–74.
Ingold, T. 2000. *Perception of the Environment: Essays in Livelihood, Dwelling and Skill*. London: Routledge.
James, E. 2000. "Rewriting the Christian Apocalypse as a Science-Fictional Event." In *Imagining Apocalypse: Studies in Cultural Crisis*, ed. D. Seed. Basingstoke: Macmillan: 54–61.
Jünger, E. 1947. *On the Marble Cliffs*. New York: New Directions.
Jünger, E. 2012. *The Adventurous Heart: Figures and Capriccios*. Candor, NY: Telos Press.
Jünger, E. 2013. *The Forest Passage*. Candor, NY: Telos Press.
Jünger, E. 2015. *Eumeswil*. Candor, NY: Telos Press.
Jünger, E. 2017. *The Worker: Dominion and Form*. Evanston, IL: Northwestern University Press.
Kaczynski, T. J. 2010. *Technological Slavery*. Port Townsend, WA: Feral House.
Klausen, J. C. 2014. *Fugitive Rousseau: Slavery, Primitivism, and Political Freedom*. New York: Fordham University Press.
Larson, S. 2000. *Captured in the Middle: Tradition and Experience in Contemporary Native American Writing*. Seattle: University of Washington Press.
Lévi-Strauss, C. 1992. *Tristes tropiques*. London: Penguin Books.

Lewis, S. 2017. "Cthulhu Plays No Role for Me." www.viewpointmag.com/2017/05/08/cthulhu-plays-no-role-for-me.

Lomax, W. 1990. "Epic Reversal in Mary Shelley's *The Last Man*: Romantic Irony and the Roots of Science Fiction." In *Contours of the Fantastic: Selected Essays from the Eighth International Conference on the Fantastic in the Arts*, ed. M. K. Langford. New York: Greenwood Press: 7–18.

Lovejoy, A. O., and Boas, G. 1935. *Primitivism and Related Ideas in Antiquity*. Baltimore: Johns Hopkins University Press.

Manjikian, M. 2012. *Apocalypse and Post-Politics: The Romance of the End*. Lanham, MD: Lexington Books.

Marder, M. 2013. *Plant-Thinking: A Philosophy of Vegetal Life*. New York: Columbia University Press.

Marx, K. 1990. *Capital*. Volume 1. London: Penguin.

Marx, K. 1993. *Grundrisse: Foundations of the Critique of Political Economy*. London: Penguin.

Marx, K. 1998. *The German Ideology*. New York: Prometheus Books.

McPherson, R. S. 2014. *Viewing the Ancestors: Perceptions of the Anaasází, Mokwič, and Hisatsinom*. Norman: University of Oklahoma Press (New Directions in Native American Studies).

Mitchell, R. G., Jr. 2002. *Dancing at Armageddon: Survivalism and Chaos in Modern Times*. Chicago: University of Chicago Press.

Morton, T. 2003. "Mary Shelley as Cultural Critic." In *The Cambridge Companion to Mary Shelley*, ed. E. Schor. Cambridge: Cambridge University Press: 259–73.

Mosby, I. 2013. *Mosby's Medical Dictionary*. 8th ed. St. Louis: Mosby/Elsevier.

Munro, L. 2013. *Archaic Style in English Literature, 1590–1674*. Cambridge: Cambridge University Press.

Nussbaum, M. 2011. *Creating Capabilities: The Human Development Approach*. Cambridge, MA: Harvard University Press.

Obrist, H. U., and Raza, A. 2017. *Mondialité, or, The Archipelagos of Édouard Glissant*. Paris: Éditions Skira.

O'Dea, G. 1992. "Prophetic History and Textuality in Mary Shelley's *The Last Man*." *Papers on Language and Literature* 28.3: 283–304.

Paley, M. D. 1993. "*The Last Man*: Apocalypse without Millennium." In *The Other Mary Shelley: Beyond* Frankenstein, eds. A. A. Fisch, A. K. Mellor, and E. H. Schor. Oxford: Oxford University Press: 107–23.

Parrinder, P. 1995. "From Mary Shelley to *The War of the Worlds*: The Thames Valley Catastrophe." In *Anticipations: Essays on Early Science Fiction and Its Precursors*, ed. D. Seed. Liverpool: University of Liverpool Press: 58–74.

Patterson, A. 1987. *Pastoral and Ideology: Virgil to Valéry*. Berkeley: University of California Press.

Pauketat, T. R. 2009. *Cahokia: Ancient America's Great City on the Mississippi*. New York: Penguin Books.
Pavel, T. G. 2013. *The Lives of the Novel: A History*. Princeton: Princeton University Press.
Payne, M. 2019. "Shared Life as Chorality in Schiller, Hölderlin, and Hellenistic Poetry." In *Antiquities Beyond Humanism*, eds. E. Bianchi, S. Brill, and B. Holmes. Oxford: Oxford University Press: 141–58.
Price, R. 1979. *Maroon Societies: Rebel Slave Communities in the Americas*. Baltimore: Johns Hopkins University Press.
Reynolds, L. J. 2005. "'Strangely Ajar with the Human Race': Hawthorne, Slavery, and the Question of Moral Responsibility." In *Hawthorne and the Real: Bicentennial Essays*, ed. M. Bell. Columbus: Ohio State University Press: 40–69.
Roberts, N. 2015. *Freedom as Marronage*. Chicago: University of Chicago Press.
Rood, T., Atack, C., and Phillips, T. 2020. *Anachronism and Antiquity*. London: Bloomsbury.
Rose, N. 2007. *The Politics of Life Itself: Biomedicine, Power, and Subjectivity in the Twenty-First Century*. Princeton: Princeton University Press.
Rousseau, J.-J. 1979. *Reveries of the Solitary Walker*. London: Penguin Books.
Rousseau, J.-J. 1997. *The Discourses and Other Early Political Writings*. Cambridge: Cambridge University Press.
Saunders, T. 2001. "Dicaearchus' Historical Anthropology." In *Dicaearchus of Messana*, ed. W. W. Fortenbaugh and E. Schütrumpf. London: Routledge (Rutgers University Studies in Classical Humanities): 237–54.
Sayre, R. F. 1977. *Thoreau and the American Indians*. Princeton: Princeton University Press.
Schiller, F. 1998. *Essays*. New York: Continuum.
Schmitt, C. 2007. *Theory of the Partisan*. New York: Telos Press.
Scott, J. C. 2017. *Against the Grain: A Deep History of the Earliest States*. New Haven: Yale University Press.
Shaw, B. D. 2001. *Spartacus and the Slave Wars: A Brief History with Documents*. Boston: Bedford / St. Martin's Press.
Shelley, P. B. 2003. *The Major Works*. Oxford: Oxford University Press.
Slusser, G. 2000. "Pocket Apocalypse: American Survivalist Fictions from *Walden* to *The Incredible Shrinking Man*." In *Imagining Apocalypse: Studies in Cultural Crisis*, ed. D. Seed. Basingstoke: Macmillan: 118–35.
Snyder, R. L. 1978. "Apocalypse and Indeterminacy in Mary Shelley's *The Last Man*." *Studies in Romanticism* 17.4: 435–52.
Sontag, S. 1961. *Against Interpretation and Other Essays*. New York: Picador.
Stabler, J. 2013. *The Artistry of Exile: Romantic and Victorian Writers in Italy*. Oxford: Oxford University Press.

Stillman, P. G. 2003. "Dystopian Critiques, Utopian Possibilities, and Human Purposes in Octavia Butler's *Parables*." *Utopian Studies* 14.1: 15–35.
Sumpter, C. 2011. "Machiavelli Writes the Future: History and Progress in Richard Jefferies's *After London*." *Nineteenth-Century Contexts* 33.4: 315–31.
Sussman, C. 2003. "'Islanded in the World': Cultural Memory and Human Mobility in *The Last Man*." *PMLA* 118.2: 286–301.
Suvin, D. 1979. *Metamorphoses of Science Fiction: On the Poetics and History of a Literary Genre*. New Haven: Yale University Press.
Suvin, D. 1983. *Victorian Science Fiction in the UK: The Discourses of Knowledge and of Power*. Boston: G. K. Hall.
Thomas, H. 2000. *Romanticism and Slave Narratives: Transatlantic Testimonies*. Cambridge: Cambridge University Press (Cambridge Studies in Romanticism).
Vaneigem, R. 1998. *The Movement of the Free Spirit: General Considerations and Firsthand Testimony Concerning Some Brief Flowerings of Life in the Middle Ages, the Renaissance and, Incidentally, Our Own Time*. New York: Zone Books.
Vaneigem, R. 2019. *A Declaration of the Rights of Human Beings: On the Sovereignty of Life as Surpassing the Rights of Man*. Oakland: PM Press.
Verhasselt, E. 2018. *Felix Jacoby: Die Fragmente der Griechischen Historiker Continued: IVB: History of Literature, Music, Art and Culture. Fascicle 9: Dikaiarchos of Messene* [No. 1400]. Leiden: Brill.
Vizenor, G. 1994. *Manifest Manners: Narratives on Postindian Survivance*. Lincoln: University of Nebraska Press.
Wagar, W. 1982. *Terminal Visions: The Literature of Last Things*. Bloomington: University of Indiana Press.
Wagar. W. 2004. *H. G. Wells: Traversing Time*. Middletown, CT: Wesleyan University Press.
Wang, F. 2011. "'We Must Live Elsewhere': The Social Construction of Natural Immunity in Mary Shelley's *The Last Man*." *European Romantic Review* 22:2: 235–55.
Webb, S. 2000. "Reading the End of the World: *The Last Man*, History, and the Agency of Romantic Authorship." In *Mary Shelley in Her Times*, eds. B. T. Bennett and S. Curran. Baltimore: Johns Hopkins University Press: 119–33.
Woolf, V. 1932. *The Second Common Reader*. New York: Harcourt.
Wynter, S. 1989. "Beyond the Word of Man: Glissant and the New Discourse of the Antilles." *World Literature Today* 63.4: 637–48.
Zerilli, L. M. G. 1994. *Signifying Woman: Culture and Chaos in Rousseau, Burke, and Mill*. Ithaca, NY: Cornell University Press.

INDEX

accounting, adversarial, 13–14, 138, 140–41, 144–47
The Adventurous Heart (Jünger), 165
African Eclogues (Chatterton), 30
After London, or Wild England (Jefferies), 14, 77–82, 106, 163
After the End (Berger), 20
agrarianism: agriculture and postapocalyptic survivalism, 2; as fatal error, 94, 97, 104; Greek culture, 26–27, 84; postapocalyptic, 77; and postapocalyptic social order, 2; regression to, 14, 44–45; and Shelley, 2, 10, 77; and social group formation, 43n10
Alas, Babylon (Frank), 100–101, 107, 110, 127, 195
alternative histories, 82, 106–7. *See also* historical imagination
Always Coming Home (Le Guin), 117–20, 172; ethnographic detail and world-building in, 75, 118; and indigenous forms of life, 117; mentation in, 7–8; as weak text, 117–19
American Indians. *See* indigenous peoples
anachronism, 48–49, 73, 124–25
animals: domestication of, 65–66, 104, 138–39, 149; human survival and dependence on, 6–7; and idea of freedom, 26–29, 32, 66; "political" animals, 136–7n14; as protagonists, 135–36. *See also* non-human life

anthropology, speculative: and Aristotle, 72; and Butler, 155n55; and capabilities theory, 23–24; and Clastres, 69–71; and Dicaearchus, 65–69; Hegland and explicit use of, 108; and Hesiod, 64; and language of defect, 71–72; and Le Guin, 76, 101, 117–18; and Lévi-Strauss, 69; and McCarthy's *The Road*, 124; postapocalyptic fiction as thought experiment, 43–44; and recovery of human capabilities, 75, 76, 79–80, 113, 161; and Rousseau, 69, 72–73, 162; and totalizing cultural simulations, 74, 137
apocalypse: and divine hostility, 2, 11–12, 46–47, 49–50, 54, 83; as environmental crisis, 1, 38–39; as global annihilation of humans, 3, 9–10, 37–38, 40; and human agency, 47, 56, 94–96, 153–54, 172–73; human persistence through, 9, 11–12, 54–56; and loss of technology, 87–88, 161–62; Nature as agent of, 12–13, 83–84; and nuclear war, 116, 125, 166; as opportunity, 23, 35, 163–64; as periodic occurrence, 2, 11, 46–48, 46–51, 54; as transformative, 13–14
Apocalypse and Post-Politics (Manjikian), 19–20
"apocalypse on trial," 7, 14–15, 25–26, 119
apocalyptic fiction, 19; popularity of, 24; *vs.* postapocalyptic fiction, 1–2

182 INDEX

Aristotle: Butler's Earthseed and, 157–58; contrasted with Rousseau, 72; on humanness and the polis, 4–5, 21, 25, 64–65; and "political animals," 136–37n; and speculation on the deep past, 72; and the study of life, 72, 157
ataraxia (freedom from care), 69, 89, 111–12
atomic period postapocalyptic fiction, 77, 97–105 min range
Atwood, Margaret, 126–27
Auster, Paul, 50, 122–23
autarky: as alternative to the State, 69–71; and *ataraxia*, 110–12; and connectivity, 113–14; and freedom, 112–13; and human capabilities, 69–70, 91; and indigenous literature, 131–35; and indigenous societies, 69–70; and postapocalyptic fiction, 69; as prosocial, 68–69, 71, 104; and satisfaction, 67, 91, 112–14; and self-sufficiency, 112–13, 138

Bellamy, Edward, 79–80, 86
Beresford, J. D., 50, 83–85
Berger, James, 20
Berman, Russell, 164
Bias of Priene, 8–9, 165
Blackwood, Algernon, 83
Blake (Delany), 32–33, 170
Blood Meridian (McCarthy), 124
The Book of Dave (Self), 19
Botany Bay Eclogues (Southey), 30
Brin, David, 16, 51, 105–7, 128–29
Buell, Lawrence, 153
Butler, Octavia, 16; and communitarian ontology, 130–31, 163; and cosmopartisans, 166–67; and Earthseed as culturecraft, 159–60; *Parable of the Sower*, 16, 130–31, 159–60, 163; shared ontology and social cohesion, 157
Butler, Samuel, 79–80

Cahokia, 170–72
California (Lepucki), 19
Canavan, Gerry, 160
A Canticle for Leibowitz (Miller), 19, 99
capabilities, human: and autarky, 69–70, 91; civilization and diminished, 14, 24–25, 66, 71–72, 77–78, 93–94, 115, 139; and experience or occupation, 3, 14, 76, 89, 94; and freedom, 67, 164–65; and hunter-gatherer culture, 94; as individual and embodied, 3; polis culture as limit to, 21, 66; postapocalyptic fiction and imagined, 2–3; postapocalyptic fiction and recovery of, 76; and Rousseau, 73–74; and self-realization, 77–81; and self-sufficiency, 5–6, 69; and social organization, 3
capabilities theory, 22–24
Capital (Marx), 4
capital punishment, 107, 127
catastrophes and catastrophism, 20, 38n, 50–51, 118, 163–67, 169
Cavell, Stanley, 141
The Centaur (Blackwood), 83
Césaire, Aimé, 33
Chamoiseau, Patrick, 31
Chatterton, Thomas, 30
children, 154
Christopher, John, 98
Cicero, 8–9, 165
cities. *See* Cahokia; the polis
civilization: agriculture and (*See* agrarianism); and diminished human capability, 14, 24–25, 66, 71–72, 77–78, 93–94, 115, 139; the polis (*See* the polis); and security, 23–24, 78, 85, 97, 104, 109; as shared performative endeavor, 107; stages or levels of, 86–87, 90–91. *See also* culturecraft
Clare, John, 28–30
Clastres, Pierre, 69–71
Collier, John, 14–15

colonialism: colonial culture, 99–103; encounters between indigenous peoples and, 78n23; and marronage, 26, 164; and popularity of pastorals, 28n25; settler culture in postapocalyptic fiction, 101, 102, 158; space travel and extraterrestrial, 166, 171
communitarianism, 50, 129, 157; autarky and collective life, 69–70; Butler and, 130–31, 163; freedom and collective life, 24–25; in survivalist fiction, 16, 129–31, 157
community: and collective imagination, 106–7; membership as contingent upon participation, 158–59; and religion, 18, 156–58; shared ontology and social cohesion, 17. *See also* sociality
The Confidence-Man (Melville), 141, 152–53
connectivity: and autarky, 113–14
cosmic consciousness, 57–62
cosmopartisans, 35–36, 163, 165–67
Cousin de Grainville, Jean-Baptiste, 18–19
Crace, Jim, 15, 120
Crèvecour, Michel-Guillaume Saint-Jean de, 102, 104, 115
Csicsery-Ronay, Istvan, 168
cultural simulation, 74, 131–33, 136–37
culturecraft, 101–2, 172; civilization, 157–60; Earthseed as, 156–60; historical imagination and, 110; posthuman, 127–28, 149; survivalism and, 127–28, 130–31, 149, 154
Curtis, Claire, 19
cycle of destruction and renewal: and civilization, 101; in *fin-de-siècle* postapocalyptic fiction, 83–84; and Hesiod, 2, 10–12; humans as doomed to, 92–93, 96–97, 104; Le Guin's adaptation as alternative to, 118; and regeneration of humankind, 9, 23–24
Cypria, 83–84, 89

The Death of Grass (Christopher), 98
A Declaration of the Rights of Human Beings (Vaneigem), 68–69
Defoe, Daniel, 3–4, 6, 102, 168
Delany, Martin, 32–33
detail, descriptive: in Le Guin's *Always Coming Home*, 75, 118; realism and, 14–15, 19, 147–48; and world building, 121n99
determinism, 106, 127; environmental, 74–75, 101–2, 172
Dicaearchus, 5, 21, 25, 28, 64–69, 89; and self-sufficiency as foundation of happiness, 69; and value of poetry, 28, 64–65, 89, 165
didacticism, 18, 46, 96, 113n87, 122–23. *See also* culturecraft
Discourse on Inequality (Rousseau), 8, 23, 43–44, 72, 93, 102, 112–13, 165
Douglass, Frederick, 31–32
Doyle, Arthur Conan, 83
dystopias, 1, 13, 19, 24

Earth Abides (Stewart), 14, 101–5, 107, 115, 118, 127
Eclogues (Virgil), 27–28, 93
ecological crisis, 1, 38, 40
economics: of imagined Golden Age, 68–70; labor and Neolithic, 114; in postapocalyptic fiction, 24, 153–54; of slave labor, 124–25; wealth hoarding and inequality, 69
Eliot, T. S., 152
embodiment, 7, 19, 32, 94, 161–62, 164–65
Enneads (Plotinus), 58–61
enslavement: escape from forced labor, 120–21; and exclusion in polis culture, 31; labor economics and inequality, 69–70; marronage and escape, 78; and sexual politics, 124–25
environmental determinism, 172
The Epic of Gilgamesh, 1

Erewhon (Butler), 79–80
ethics, eschatological *vs.* survival, 19
extraterrestrials, 121, 166, 171

The Falcon (Tanner), 115
Far North (Theroux), 120–21
fin-de-siècle postapocalyptic fiction, 77–85
fire, 47, 111–12, 121–22, 151, 154
Fiskadoro (Johnson), 19, 98–99
foraging, 14, 76
forest fleer figure, 35–36, 163–65
The Forest Passage (Jünger), 163–65
Forster, E. M., 161–62
Frank, Pat, 100–101
Frankenstein (Shelley), 40–41, 122
freedom: animal behavior and instantiation of idea of, 26–30, 29–30, 32, 66; *ataraxia* (freedom from care), 69, 89, 111–12; autarky and self-sufficiency, 112–13; Clare and poetic, 28–29; and dependence, 69–71; as embodied understanding, 32; and ethicality, 164–65; and human capabilities, 67, 164–65; in indigenous stories, 172; individual *vs.* collective, 78n22; Jünger's "forest flight" (*Waldgänger*) and, 35–36, 163–65; marronage as form of, 26–27, 30, 34, 78–79; in Mitchell's time travel novels, 92; Nature and, 8–9, 30, 31; non-human life and understanding of, 29–30; and pastorals, 24–25, 27–30; polis culture and loss of, 24–25; political, 28, 30, 32–34; postapocalyptic fiction and imagined, 2–3; and security, 78, 93, 97, 104, 108–9; shared life as constraint, 138–39, 151–52; space as necessary for, 30–31, 33–34, 78, 163, 166; and the state, 69–71; Vaneigem and rights tradition as memory of, 68; in Virgil's *Eclogues*, 27
frontier mentality, 160–61

fugitivity, 30–31, 164–67; and Jünger's "forest fleer," 164n1; and self-sufficiency, 165
Full Circle (Collier), 14–15

Gay Hunter (Mitchell), 14, 93, 95–97
The German Ideology (Marx), 5–6
Ghosh, Amitav, 38–40, 45–46, 50–51, 92
"glissading": authorial choice of stopping point, 76–77, 88, 100, 105–6, 118, 120–21, 125; defined, 48–49; regression to agrarian life, 44–45; as repeated or cyclical, 90–91, 172; technological regression in Shank's *The People of the Ruins*, 48–59, 86–87
Glissant, Edouard, 33–34
Golden Age: as autarkic, 67–71; Dicaearchus on the, 65–69; economy of, 68–70; as folk memory of Deep History, 89, 93–95, 104; Hesiod's account of, 2, 10–11, 65, 69; Lao-Tze and Daoist, 94–95; poetry or poetic fictions and imagined, 25, 89, 94–95; Rousseau and recall of, 75; and social bonds, 70–71; speculative Neolithic as, 94–95; as utopian future, 80; Vaneigem and rights tradition as memory of, 68
Golden Days (See), 116
Goslings (Beresford), 50, 83–85
The Great God Pan (Machen), 83
Greek culture: and agrarianism, 26–27, 84; as inspiration, 106–7; and relationship with Nature, 83–84; and religious mythology, 10, 44–45, 53, 81, 83–84, 104; slavery in, 26–27; and three-stage model of human history, 25, 65–66 (*See also* Golden Age). *See also* the polis
Grundrisse (Marx), 4–5

Hamilton, Cicely, 14, 88–96, 104, 125
happiness, 14, 18, 64; capabilities theory and, 22–23; and Golden Age

mythology of the past, 104;
Kaczynski on, 115; and postapocalyptic freedom, 35–36; and self-sufficiency, 67–70; and survival, 68
Haraway, Donna, 168–69
Hawthorne, Nathaniel, 9, 17, 83, 142–47, 171
Hay, John, 20
Heffernen, Teresa, 20
Hegland, Jean, 14, 108
Heise, Ursula, 1
Heraclitus, 58, 156–57
Hesiod: and cyclical destruction and renewal, 10–12, 54, 64; and divine hostility, 2, 11, 46–47, 54; and human capability, 11; and humanness as persistent, 17–18, 48; and knowledge preservation, 54; and negative exceptionalism, 54; road as motif in, 15–16, 50; and Shelley's *The Last Man*, 2, 10–12, 18, 37–38, 40; and speculative anthropology, 64; and successive versions of humankind, 1–2, 10–11, 14–15, 65, 69, 99; as traveling observer, 51
Hicks, Heather, 20
historical imagination, 82, 110. See also speculative anthropology
history, human: as cyclical, 6, 13; fixation on the past, 131–32; Greek three-stage model of, 6, 25, 65–66 (*See also* Golden Age); poetry and memory of deep, 64–68, 75, 90–91, 93, 165. *See also* anthropology, speculative
Holn, Nathan, 106
hubris, 47n17
humanness: and arrested development, 43–44; and mentation, 13–14, 46–47, 50–51, 126; as persistent through change, 14, 17–18, 48, 54–63; polis civilization as prerequisite for, 72; and rational perfectibility, 20; and sociality, 4–5;

social life as foundational to, 12; Stapledon's eighteen kinds of human beings, 54–56, 61
hunting and gathering, 14, 64, 76
Hymn to Demeter (Callimachus), 42–43

I Am Legend (Matheson), 16–17, 102–4, 129, 147–49
Idylls (Theocritus), 28
"In Defence of Poetry" (Shelley), 51–53
indigenous literature: and autarky, 131–35; and environmental determinism, 172; exploration and the future in oral tradition, 171–72; freedom in, 172; McNickle's *The Surrounded*, 5, 131–35, 137; McNickle's *Wind from an Enemy Sky*, 170; and oral tradition, 76, 171–72; as postapocalyptic fiction, 130–31; and reparative cathexis, 131–33, 137–38; and survivance, 74, 131–34, 137; Welch's *Winter in the Blood*, 5–6, 135–38
indigenous peoples: American Indians as postapocalyptic people, 130–31; Atwood's Crakers, 126–27; and autarky, 69–70, 131–35; Hawthorne's Sagamore, 145–46; and knowledge, 100–101, 103–4, 117–18; and nonhuman life, 136–7n14; reservation life, 5–6, 20, 131–35; stories of (*See* indigenous literature); Vizenor and ethnographic totalizing of indigenous cultures and survivance, 74
individualism, 34, 43n10, 78n22
industrial civilization, 38–39, 86, 94–95, 101
inequality, 1, 8; and biopolitics of slavery, 124–25; and civilization, 66; hierarchical caste systems, 81, 93; and surplus as cause of covetousness, 65–66, 70
interiority, 9, 18, 77, 96

interwar period postapocalyptic fiction, 77, 85–97
In the Country of Lost Things (Auster), 50, 122–23
Into the Forest (Hegland), 14, 108–13, 115–18, 155, 162
Ishi, 101, 116

Jefferies, Richard, 14, 72–82
Johnson, Denis, 19, 98–99
Juana Maria, Lone Woman of San Nicolas Island, 116
Jünger, Ernst, 35, 163–65, 170

Kaczynski, Theodore, 114–15
Kareiva, Peter, 1
Klausen, Jimmy Casas, 30, 78
knowledge: acquired by osmosis, 122–23; autarky and wisdom, 67; books or libraries and transmission of, 100–103, 106–10, 155; and didacticism, 96; as experiential, 3–4, 90–91, 96, 123; loss of, 123; and memory, 123; mortal limits of, 146; poetry and remembered, 94; skills and community formation, 158; subsistence skills as, 5–6. *See also* culturecraft; technology

Lao-Tze, 94
Larson, Sidner, 130
Last and First Men (Stapledon), 13, 54–63
last-man narratives, 19, 37, 54
The Last Man (Shelley), 9–13; critical reception of, 12, 51, 53; and Hesiod as model, 2, 10–12, 18, 37–38, 40; narrative structure of, 40–43; Nature in, 40, 53–54; occupation and mentation in, 10, 12–13, 18, 44, 53–54; and speculative fiction/genre, 37; temporality in, 39n3; as weak text, 40–42
last survivors, 19, 40–42, 123. *See also The Last Man* (Shelley)

Laws (Plato), 54, 64
Le dernier homme (Cousin de Grainville), 18–19
Lee, Chang-Rae, 19
"Legends for a New Land" (Le Guin), 119–20
Le Guin, Ursula: *Always Coming Home* by, 7–8, 75, 117–20, 172; ethnographic detail and world-building by, 75, 118; and immersion in the future, 118–20; and regressive mode of speculative fiction, 76; and speculative anthropology, 76, 101, 117–18
Lepucki, Edan, 19
Lessing, Doris, 19, 98
Lest Ye Die (Hamilton). *See Theodore Savage* (Hamilton)
Lévi-Strauss, Claude, 35, 69–72
Lewis, Sophie, 169
The Life of Greece (Dicaearchus), 5, 21, 25, 64–69
logic of belief, 98–99
London, Jack, 83
Looking Backward (Bellamy), 79–80, 86
Lost Empire (Holn), 106
Lovecraft, H. P., 169

The Mable Faun (Hawthorne), 83
Machen, Arthur, 83
"The Machine Stops" (Forster), 161–62
MaddAddam (Atwood), 126–27, 167
Mandel, Emily St. John, 15, 19
Manifest Manners (Vizenor), 74–75
Manjikian, Mary, 19–20
"The Man Who Became a Tree" (Stapledon), 57–58
Markson, David, 19
maroons and marronage, 6, 42, 169–70; and freedom, 26–27, 30, 34, 78–79, 163–64; and Greek herdsmen slaves, 26–27; in Jefferies's *After London*, 79–80, 88, 162; maroons as figures, 26, 33, 34, 36, 78, 163–64; and pastorals, 26–27, 34; and

self-realization, 78–80, 167; and space of freedom, 30–31, 78, 166; and space travel, 162
Martin, John, 37n
Marx, Karl, 4–5, 25
Matheson, Richard, 16–17, 102, 129, 147–49
McCarthy, Cormac, 15–16, 50, 121–29, 154
McGann, Jerome, 33, 170
McNickle, D'Arcy, 5, 131–35, 137, 170
Melville, Herman, 141, 152–53
The Memoirs of a Survivor (Lessing), 19, 98
memory: and experiential knowledge, 96; "ghost" memories of the deep past, 94; memory loss as trope, 122; occupation and recovery of, 117; poetry and deep history, 64–68, 75, 90, 93–94, 165; and reparative cathexis, 131–33, 137–38
mentation: and apocalypse, 9; catastrophism, 50–51; cosmic consciousness, 57–62; defined, 7; as determined by occupation, 14, 44–45, 110–11; and embodiment, 7, 94, 161–62, 164–65; as human capability, 13–14, 46–47, 50–51, 126; social groups and collective, 10, 105–6; survival conditions and changed, 7–8, 16–17, 53–54, 128–29; vegetal thinking, 65
Miller, Walter M., 19, 99
Mitchell, Leslie, 14, 95
Mitchell, Richard G., 130–31
Morris, William, 79–80
mortality, 145–46
The Movement of the Free Spirit (Vaneigem), 82
music, 73, 103–4; and preservation of human knowledge, 96; in Stapledon's works, 57–63
My Bondage and My Freedom (Douglass), 31

narrative: cognitive signaling as device, 61; frameworks, 38; as insulating or mediating framework, 38; structure of Shelley's *The Last Man*, 40–43; weak texts and found manuscripts, 41–43, 47–48, 50, 142
natural life: and *ataraxia* (freedom from care), 69, 111; survival and reconstitution of self, 8–9
Nature: as agent of human destruction, 83–84; Culture/Nature boundary, 39–40; in Heraclitus, 58; and human capability, 33–34; human dependence on, 44–45, 83, 132; and humans as parasitic infection, 83; as living home of humans, 58–59; Pan, 83–84; in Plotinus, 58–59; poets and representation of, 51–53; and recovery of freedom, 33–34; and recovery of human capability, 94; as setting, 39–40; in Shelley's *The Last Man*, 12, 39–40; state-of-nature theorists, 19–20; survivalism and adversarial relationship with, 138–39; in Thoreau's *Walden*, 137–41
near-future dystopias, 19
Neolithic: as Golden Age, 114; as Kaczynski's ideal, 114–15; Lévi-Strauss on "speculative," 72–73; in Mitchell's time travel novels, 93–96; regression to, 100–101; as Roussean ideal, 69–74, 93; in Stewart's *Earth Abides*, 103–4; as vision of future, 161
News from Nowhere (Morris), 79–80
"A Non-Euclidean View of California as A Cold Place to Be" (Le Guin), 76
non-human life: as adversaries in survivalist fiction, 129–30; animals (*See* animals); anthropomorphism and, 39–40; Aristotle and attention to, 136n14, 157; connection with and reality of, 134–35; and dehumanization of humans, 150–51; and the future, 125; human survival and

non-human life (*continued*)
dependence on, 6–7; and imaginary violence, 139–40; ontological distanciation from, 16–17; plants and vegetal life in Stapledon, 57–63; posthumans in survivalist fiction, 16–17, 126–27, 147–49, 153, 167; and sense of shared life, 162; speculative anthropology and connectivity with, 113; transgenic, 126–27, 167; vampires and zombies in fiction, 16–17, 129, 147–54

nuclear war, 98–99, 116, 166. *See also* atomic period postapocalyptic fiction

Nussbaum, Martha, 22

occupation and mentation: in Auster's *In the Country of Last Things*, 122–23; in Brin's *The Postman*, 105–6; in Defoe's *Robinson Crusoe*, 3–5; as disconnected, 98–99; and indigenous knowledge, 103–4; in Jefferies's *After London*, 77–79; Le Guin's "hand-mind" as expression of relationship between, 7–8; in McNickle's *The Surrounded*, 131–35; mentation as determined by occupation, 14, 44–45, 110–11; in Shelley's *The Last Man*, 10, 12–13, 18, 44, 53–54; and speculative anthropology, 75–76; in Stapledon's novels, 13–15; in Stewart's *Earth Abides*, 116–17; and survival, 3–4, 7–8, 9, 16–17, 53–54, 128–29; Vizenor's survivance, 74–75

"On Naïve and Sentimental Poetry" (Schiller), 43n9, 51–52, 76

On Such a Full Sea (Lee), 19

On the Beach (Shute), 99–100

On the Marble Cliffs (Jünger), 163–65

Oryx and Crake (Atwood), 126–27, 126–28

Pan (mythological figure), 83–84

Parable of the Sower (Butler), 16; and communitarian ontology, 130–31; 163; and Earthseed as culturecraft, 159–60; as survivalist fiction, 16, 130

Parable of the Talents (Butler), 159–60

Parts of Animals (Aristotle), 157

pastoral: as cultural memory, 93; and freedom, 27–34; and landscape as imaginative space, 13; and marronage, 26–27; postapocalyptic fiction as, 24–25, 34, 169; science fiction's similarity to pastoral poetry, 24–25; as speculative past, 76; and Theocritus, 27

Patterson, Annabel, 28

The People of the Ruins (Shanks), 15–16, 48–49, 85–88

The Pesthouse (Crace), 15, 120

Philoctetes (Sophocles), 6, 42–43

phthonos (ill-will), 12, 54

pirates, 120, 166–67

place, 10; environmental determinism, 101–2, 172; and forms of sociality, 23; urban life, 24, 130, 170–71

Plato, 54, 64

Plotinus, 58–61

poetry, 5; and catastrophism, 37–38; Dicaearchus and value of, 28, 64–65, 89, 165; and freedom, 33–34; juridical role of, 51–53; and memory of deep history, 64–68, 75, 90, 93–94, 165; and representation of Nature, 51–53; and song in Hamilton's *Gay Hunter*, 96; and speculative anthropology, 64

The Poison Belt (Doyle), 83

the polis: in *After London*, 81–82; and compulsory social relations, 24; destruction of the metropolis in *fin-de-siècle* fiction, 82–83; enslavement and exclusion in, 31; and humanness, 4–5, 21, 25, 64–65, 72; and intrusion on private life, 164; and security, 23–24. *See also* Cahokia

politics: autarky as alternative to the State, 69–71; biopolitics of slavery and inequality, 124–25; communitarianism, 50, 130–31; hierarchical castes and systemic inequality, 81, 93; human rights, 68; local resistance to global ideology, 166; postapocalyptic fiction as political theory, 2–3; postapocalyptic fiction as thought experiment, 43–44, 92; post-state scenarios in fiction, 20; and the social contract, 5; and social inequality as inevitable, 95; solitary survivalism, 50, 107, 130; woman as figure in Western political theory, 167–68

Politics (Aristotle), 72

Post-Apocalyptic Culture (Heffernan), 20

Postapocalyptic Fantasies in Antebellum American Literature (Hay), 20

postapocalyptic fiction: and autarky, 69; contrasted with near-future dystopias, 24; and freedom, 25–26, 34; history of genre, 2, 37; and novel forms of sociality, 21; as opportunity for imagining freedom, sociality, capability, 2–3; positivity in, 20–21, 45; as prosocial, 25–26, 34, 69; and realization of potential, 120; and recovery of human capabilities, 75–76; and "stalled" dialectic, 160–61

Postapocalyptic Fiction and the Social Contracts (Curtis), 18

The Post-Apocalyptic Novel in the Twenty-First Century (Hicks), 20

posthumans, 16–17, 147–49, 153, 167

The Postman (Brin), 16, 51, 105–7, 128–29

Pound, Ezra, 152

Price, Richard, 26

Prometheus, 48, 121–22

The Purple Cloud (Shiel), 53, 82–83, 101

readers: and ethnographic details, 75; and mediation by weak text, 40–42; mutual companionship with author, 119; popularity of apocalyptic fiction, 1–3; and vicarious "apocalypse on trial" experience, 7, 14–15, 25–26, 119

realism, 14–15, 19; and descriptive detail in postapocalyptic fictions, 121–22; didactic realism, 122–23; vs. speculative fiction, 37–38, 92

regeneration: and apocalypse, 23–24; and isolation or solitude, 21; and vegetal thinking, 65

regression, cultural, 41–42; and frontier mentality, 161; and slavery, 124–25. See also "glissading"

religion, 9; as consoling fiction, 53; cosmologies and cycles of destruction, 46–47; divine hostility as cause of apocalypse, 2, 11–12, 40, 46–47, 49–50, 54, 83; divine indifference or boredom, 62–63; Greek mythology, 10, 44–45, 53, 81, 83–84; Noah story as apocalyptic fiction, 1, 11; and occupation, 44–45; in Octavia Butler's *Parable*, 156; postapocalyptic fiction and, 20

reservation literature. See indigenous literature

return of the past, 16, 77, 88–91, 105

Reveries of the Solitary Walker (Rousseau), 112–13, 162

rewilding, 98

The Road (McCarthy), 15–16, 154; and historical memory, 121, 124–25; as survivalist fiction, 124

roads (the road): in Beresford's *Goslings*, 83–85; in Hesiod's *Works and Days*, 14–15, 50; in Le Guin's *Always Coming Home*, 117–18; as marker of civilization, 86, 98; in McCarthy's *The Road*, 124–25; and narrative time, 98; as place of self-discovery, 117–18; and "precarious transport" (axles, wagons, carts), 15–16, 50, 85, 121; as relic, 85, 87–88, 120–21; in Shanks's *The People of the Ruins*, 86–88; as site of exposure, 14–15, 85, 100, 120–21

Roberts, Neil, 31, 78
Robinsonade: history of form, 7, 168; Marx and dismissal of, 4–5; reader engagement in, 7; and return to civilization, 6
Robinson Crusoe (Defoe), 43, 168; and capitalism, 4, 7; occupation and mentation in, 3–5; and Stewart's *Earth Abides*, 102. *See also* Robinsonade
Rousseau, Jean-Jacques, 5, 8, 23, 43–44, 72, 93, 102, 112–13, 120, 161–62, 165
Rushton, Edward, 30

Sahlins, Marshall, 114
satisfaction: autarky and contentment, 67, 91, 112–14
The Scarlet Plague (London), 83
scavenging, 121–22
Schiller, Friedrich, 51–52, 76
Schmitt, Carl, 35–36, 163, 165–67
security: freedom sacrificed for, 78, 93, 97, 104, 108–9; and polis culture and, 23–24; and social bonds, 70–71, 125
See, Carolyn, 116
Self, Will, 19
self-realization: civilization as obstacle to, 78–80; and doubts about identity, 80; and marronage, 78–80, 167
self-sufficiency, 91, 113; and fugitivity, 165; and happiness, 67–70; and sociality, 5
Sen, Amartya, 22
Septimius Felton/Septimus Norton, or the Elixir of Life (Hawthorne), 17, 142–45
sex, 83–84, 91–92, 99, 102, 124–25, 128, 148–49
Shanks, Edward, 15–16, 48–49, 85–88
Shaw, Brent, 30
Shelley, Mary: *Frankenstein* by, 40–41, 122; and Hesiod, 2, 10–12, 18, 37–38, 40; *The Last Man* by, 2, 9–13, 18, 37–44, 51, 53–54

Shelley, Percy Bysshe, 51–53, 93
The Shepherd's Calendar (Clare), 29–30
Shiel, M. P., 53
Shield of Heracles (Hesiod), 40
Shute, Nevil, 99–100
silence, 6n8, 27, 31, 119
"silver fork" novels, 92, 99
slave narratives, 27n24, 30–32, enslavement. *See also* maroons and marronage
Slave Old Man (Chamoiseau), 31
slavery, 124–25. *See also* maroons and marronage
Slusser, George, 129–30, 137–38
sociality: autarky as prosocial capability, 68–69, 71, 104; catastrophe and human, 18; communitarian (*See* communitarianism); and companionship, 43; and mentation, 10, 84, 105–6; parent/child dyad as nuclear unit, 125; as performative in nature, 105; polis culture (*See* polis); postapocalyptic fiction and social theory, 2–3, 19–20, 24; security and social organization, 70–71, 125; and self-sufficiency, 5; social cohesion and survival, 5, 131
Society Against the State (Clastres), 69–71
solitary survival, 50, 107; Juana Maria, Lone Woman of San Nicolas Island, 116. *See also* survivalism
Southey, Robert, 30
sovereignty. *See* autarky
space: apocalyptic destruction and clearing of, 34; as necessary for freedom, 30–31; and postapocalyptic fiction, 19
space travel (extraterrestrial colonization): and extraterrestrial colonization, 166, 171; as marronage, 162
speculative anthropology: and connectivity with nonhuman life, 113; and

optimal cultural development, 43–44; and regression as correction, 79–80
Stapledon, Olaf, 13, 18, 57, 61–63; and music as figure of humanness, 56–63
Star Maker (Stapledon), 13, 57, 61–63
Station Eleven (Mandel), 15, 19, 51
Stewart, George, 14, 101–4, 107, 115
Stoicism, 8, 69
The Surrounded (McNickle), 5, 131–35, 137
survivalism, 16, 50; and absolute self, 138–39, 142–43; and adversarial accounting, 140–41, 144–47; and "culturecraft," 127–28, 130–31, 149, 154; and killing as occupation, 16–17; and McCarthy's *The Road*, 124; negative stereotypes in postapocalyptic fiction, 16, 128; and ontological practice of separation, 129; and "prepping," 127, 148, 155; and sacrifice of others, 129, 139–40, 144–47, 155; solitary *vs.* communitarian, 16; and Thoreau's *Walden*, 129–30
survivance, 74–75, 131–34, 132–34, 137
Suvin, Darko, 24–26, 76n20

Tanner, John, 115
technology, 6n7; as burden on humanity, 95–96; dependence on, 54; and "glissading" cultural regression, 48–49, 86–87; Hesiod and preservation of, 48; as human characteristic, 95; loss of knowledge and decline of, 85, 86–87, 95; in Mitchell's *Gay Hunter*, 95; tool use as human fundamental, 48–49; and utopian futurism, 86. *See also* knowledge
temporality: anachronism, 48–49; in Hesiod, 48; and identity, 80; and reader's imagination, 48; roads and narrative time, 98; in Shelley's *The Last Man*, 39n3; time travel, 48, 80, 85–86, 93–97

Terminal Visions: The Literature of Last Things (Wagar), 20–21, 45, 77
Theocritus, 26–28
Theodore Savage (Hamilton), 14, 88–96, 104, 125
Theogony (Hesiod), 10
Theory of the Partisan (Schmitt), 163, 165–66
Theroux, Marcel, 120–21
Thoreau, Henry David: and adversarial accounting, 138, 140–41; and survivalism, 137–41; *Walden*, 17, 43, 129–31, 137–41, 144, 146–47, 153
Three Go Back (Mitchell), 14, 93–97
time (temporality): anachronisms, 48–49, 73, 124–25; past as prediction of future, 88
time travel, 48, 80, 85–86, 93–97
"To Toussaint L'Ouverture" (Wordsworth), 32
travelers: Grand Tours and survivor figures, 101–2; and point of view, 51–52; road as danger to, 120
Tristes tropiques (Lévi-Strauss), 35

urban life. *See* the polis
utopian fictions, 24, 68, 75n19, 79–80, 86

vampire and zombie fiction, 16–17, 129, 147–54
Vaneigem, Raoul, 68–69, 82
violence: capital punishment, 107, 127; in Hawthorne's *Septimius Felton*, 144, 146–47; and hunting culture, 68; killing as occupation, 16–17; and regeneration, 160; road as site of, 15–16; and survivalism, 149, 151; therapeutic, 138–40, 144, 147, 149–51
Virgil, 27–28, 93
Vizenor, Gerald, 74–75, 132

Wagar, Warren, 20–21, 45, 77, 92n47
The Wake (Kingsnorth), 82

Walden (Thoreau), 17, 43, 129–31, 137–41, 144, 146–47, 153
weak texts, 41–43, 47–48, 50
weird fiction, 83
Welch, James, 5–6, 135–38
Wells, H. G., 92
West Indian Eclogues (Rushton), 30
When Species Meet (Haraway), 168
Whitehead, Colson, 16–17
Wind from an Enemy Sky (McNickle), 170
Winter in the Blood (Welch), 5–6, 135–38
Wittgenstein's Mistress (Markson), 19
Woolf, Virginia, 3–4
Wordsworth, William, 32

Works and Days (Hesiod): as assemblage, 47–48, 50; and catastrophism, 50–51; and didactic purpose, 46; humankind as serial "ages," 11; as postapocalyptic fiction, 1–2; Shelley as influenced by, 11–12; and technology, 48–49; as weak text, 47–48
world-building, 98–99
"A World of Sound" (Stapledon), 59–60

Zerilli, Linda, 167
zombie and vampire fiction, 16–17, 129, 147–54
Zone One (Whitehead), 16–17, 129, 150–55, 160

A NOTE ON THE TYPE

This book has been composed in Arno, an Old-style serif typeface in the classic Venetian tradition, designed by Robert Slimbach at Adobe.

GPSR Authorized Representative: Easy Access System Europe - Mustamäe tee 50, 10621 Tallinn, Estonia, gpsr.requests@easproject.com

www.ingramcontent.com/pod-product-compliance
Lightning Source LLC
Chambersburg PA
CBHW020411230426
43664CB00009B/1255